the
QUIET QUARTER

the QUIET QUARTER

anthology of
new Irish writing

edited by
EOIN BRADY

NEW
ISLAND

Quiet Quarter
First published 2004
by New Island
2 Brookside
Dundrum Road
Dublin 14
www.newisland.ie

ISBN 1 904301 62 2

Typeset by New Island
Cover painting: Poppy II by Pat Harris, www.patharris.info
Cover design by Fidelma Slattery @ New Island
Printed in the UK by Mackays of Chatham Ltd

New Island received financial assistance from
The Arts Council (An Chomhairle Ealaíon), Dublin, Ireland

10 9 8 7 6 5 4 3 2 1

CONTENTS

Foreword ix

PLACE

Dermot Somers   *Deer*   •3
Gréagóir Ó Dúill   *Snail*   •6
Cathal Ó Searcaigh   *Home*   •9
Nuala Ní Chonchuir   *The River*   •12
Rose Mary Logue   *Poor Slough*   •15
Frank Corcoran   *The Sound of Exile*   •18
Pat Falvey   *The Highest Place on Earth*   •21
Paolo Tullio   *Food and Nationality*   •23
Mary Arrigan   *Dogo Onsen*   •26
Patrick Treacy   *Photograph*   •29
Martin Ryan   *Thoughts in a Kenyan Cemetery*   •32
Marguerite MacCurtain   *San Juan Chamula*   •35
Kate Thompson   *Holidays*   •38
Gerry Galvin   *Food from the Wild*   •41
Éamonn Ó Catháin   *Lyon*   •44
Alannah Hopkin   *Swimming round the Island*   •47
Peter Philips   *Niagara Falls*   •50
Chuck Kruger   *The Fastnet Lighthouse*   •53
Mae Leonard   *The King of Kilkerrin Castle*   •56
Thomas Pakenham   *Irish Giants at Risk*   •59
Fred Johnston   *The Claddagh*   •62
Kate Duignan   *Galway Rain*   •65
Margaret Lee   *The Call of the Mountains*   •68
Donal O'Kelly   *Mosney*   •71
Kevin Connolly   *Trees*   •74
Edward Denniston   *Midlands*   •77
Carl Tighe   *Living in the Irish Sea*   •80

PEOPLE

Máiride Woods *Death and Memory* •85

Mary O'Donnell *Stones* •88

Ken Bruen *I Never Sang for my Father* •91

Michael Murtagh *Forty-Four* •94

John F. Deane *I My Father on Achill Island* •97

George Szirtes *Football with the Ancestors* •100

Mary J. Byrne *The Sewing Machine* •103

Berni Dwan *A Handy Tool* •106

John Quinn *Two Ladies of Galway* •109

Anthony Jordan *Christmas 1987* •112

Rita Ann Higgins *Kate's Mother* •114

Carlo Gébler *Writer-in-Residence* •116

Sam McAughtry *The Pools Winner* •119

Geraldine Mills *My Father's Legacy* •122

Leo Cullen *The Stars* •124

Theodore Deppe *Guillemots* •127

Celia de Fréine *Rule of Thumb* •129

Tony Flannery *Sister* •132

Conor O'Callaghan *Little Man* •135

Mary P. Wilkinson *Bell* •138

Nicola Lindsay *A Life Lived* •141

Peter Cunningham *Holly* •144

Seán Ó Riain *Night-Time in the Simon Community* •147

LANGUAGE

Moya Cannon *Oughterard Lemons* •153

Iggy McGovern *The Gravity of Poetry* •156

Mark Roper *Prayer* •159

Bernard Share *Home Words from Abroad* •162

Patricia Nolan *All in a Language* •165

Mary Coll *Letters* •168

Judith Mok *The Tango People* •171

George Swede   *La Muerte on TV (A Haibun)*   •174

Pat Boran   *Stars*   •177

Ciaran O'Driscoll   *Edward Thomas and the Owl*   •180

Vincent Woods   *Lunar Landing*   •183

Peter van de Kamp   *I Love Me*   •186

Thomas F. Walsh   *Kindergarten*   •189

THE PAST

Ellen O'Toole   *Silence in Wicklow*   •195

Brian Leyden   *Tom Swift and the Amazing AI Man*   •198

Frank Marshall   *Smoking*   •200

Gabriel Fitzmaurice   *Ring out the Old, Ring in the New*   •203

Dermot Bolger   *Fatherhood*   •206

G.V. Whelan   *Wolves*   •210

Michael Coady   *Dream-Time on the Cape Shore*   •213

Rowan Hand   *The Comet*   •216

Daniel Mulhall   *The Passing of a Millennium*   •219

Sylvia Cullen   *The Hogget*   •222

John Trolan   *Cream Cakes*   •225

Joe Kearney   *Corner Boys*   •228

Gerry McDonnell   *Cinemas*   •231

Mary Mulvihill   *Spades*   •234

Eamonn Kelly   *Making up a Future*   •237

MUSIC AND SILENCE

Paddy Bushe   *When the World Holds Its Breath*   •241

Mike Absalom   *Time, Like an Ever Rolling Stone*   •244

Micheal O'Siadhail   *Jazz*   •247

Mickey McConnell   *Learning Trad*   •250

Danny Morrison   *Camping with Schubert*   •253

Noirín Ní Riain   *The Rest Is Silence*   •256

John Wakeman   *The Julian Meetings*   •259

William Wall   *Mary over Minerva*   •262

Michael Harding *Silence* •265
Kerrie Hardie *On Noise and Speed* •268
Brendan Lynch *Inevitability of the Car* •271
Michael Cronin *The Tyranny of Speed* •274

FAITH

Eamon Morrissey *Compass* •279
Enda Wyley *The Dark Hope* •281
Dick Warner *Deep Ecology and the Oak Tree* •284
Macdara Woods *The Anatomy of Silence* •286
Mark Granier *Out Far, in Deep* •289
Declan Burke *It's Only a Game* •292
Anthony Glavin *Occasions of Faith* •295
Mary Morrissy *Travelling Light* •298
Martin Drury *Suspended Belief* •300
Leland Bardwell *Suburban Idyll* •304

FOREWORD

I have always loved essays. Like short stories, they can be succinct enough to read and digest in one sitting, yet the best of them reverberate in the mind long after the pages are closed. Phrases, ideas and images from a good writer are literally food for thought, sustaining the mind during the routine tasks of the day. This is the aim of the *Quiet Quarter* radio essay series, which has been running in RTÉ lyric fm's mid-morning programme *Lyric Notes* since the station first began broadcasting. Máire Nic Gearailt – who presents the programme – and I wanted to give people an excuse each day to pause in what they were doing and hear the interesting thoughts of others. Other peoples' thoughts are usually interesting, I think: sometimes funny, sometimes sad, sometimes provocative, but almost always engaging. This is particularly true when you hear the authors themselves reading what they have written, as they do on the *Quiet Quarter*, and the series has been home to a vast range of accents and inflections every week. Unfortunately, these are difficult to duplicate on the printed page.

But what the ninety-two authors in this collection prove is the extraordinary breadth and quality of writing in Ireland today. Radio is an unforgiving medium: you only get to say your piece once and, if you lose a listener for a moment, that moment is lost forever. All of the essays in this book hold the attention, as pieces not just to be heard but also to be read. And I am gratified that every author commissioned invested their time and thought into writing pieces that have this enduring quality, even though each was ostensibly to have a life of only three and a half minutes.

When thinking of radio, I conjure up an image of a baby bird in a nest, head up-turned and beak constantly agape, no matter how much food its parents give it; as a medium, radio has a voracious maw, always demanding to be filled, never full. We have featured more than one hundred and fifty authors in the series in the past five years, every one writing five pieces, and new commissions are offered weekly. It was not easy at all to reduce this book to ninety-two writers, each represented by only one essay, and ultimately it was a subjective choice. My thanks, however, to Máire Nic Gearailt for reminding me of pieces that had slipped to the back of my mind and for acting as a sounding board for what to include. Thank you, too, to everyone who worked on the *Quiet Quarter* with us since it began, recording and editing so many of the contributors: Kevin Brew, Jean Ní Bhaoill, Martina McGlynn, Michael O'Kane, Eoghan O'Sullivan and Eoin O'Kelly.

Eoin Brady

PLACE

DEER

Dermot Somers

Dermot Somers, writer, broadcaster and mountaineer, was born in 1947. He has published two collections of fiction and a mountaineering memoir and has written and presented many television documentaries. He was a member of a successful Irish Everest expedition, 1993.

In a single day on the Arctic ice we covered sixty kilometres. The nomads of Northern Siberia were migrating to their summer pastures. The wooden sleds carrying the families were hauled by transport-reindeer, with the main herd, six thousand strong, following behind.

First there was a frozen estuary, forty kilometres; then we left the ice and took to the land. Our rhythmic team of transport-deer became a wallowing tangle, bucking and slewing

• 3 •

in bottomless snow, eyes rolling, tongues extended. It was frozen marshland, a sieve of pits and tussocks without foundation.

I was travelling with Sergei, boss of the brigade. We had six sleds haltered together in a line, each hauled by a pair of deer. A cargo of timber, hardware and furs. I held on at angles that defied gravity in several planes at once. I tried walking. Impossible: I sank to the thighs in the voids beneath the snow and stayed there, floundering.

The deer worked it somehow on their bellies, tunnelling in troughs, then lurching steeply over solid obstacles to plunge hopelessly on the other side while the sled was still mounting. It would slump cruelly on their mired haunches, catching them always on the bone. And there was no lateral consistency: while one heroic animal was heaving upwards, the creature beside it was tumbling into a trough, the sled slewing on a single runner.

The third sled in the convoy, a load of logs, overturned constantly. I'd shout a warning to Sergei and vault back across the intervening deer to rock it back on its runners, then plough back to my impossible seat. When the lead-sled jolted into motion, the sharp shock transferred through the rawhide halters to the necks of the deer all down the line. They'd lurch frantically for a footing, and for a dreadful moment the strain between any two sleds was borne by the stretch in a reindeer's neck. Their heads were within inches of my knees. I avoided eye contact, certain they held me responsible. But transport-deer make no complaint at all.

After the marsh there was solid ground. Hooves pumped again like pistons, runners bit crisply in the snow and the caravan surged, full flight, towards the spring pastures.

The deer about me had regained their rhythm and their poise – mouths closed, eyes calm, as if the débâcle behind us had never happened. There was a sense of purpose, a homing surge, a theme reaching for conclusion; small hills rose and fell, thickets of brushwood appeared, flashed past, fell back. The sun plummeted in the sky behind us; the horizon leapt to meet it, dropped again; the sun grew bigger in descent, turned to honey, promised gold.

And now the loose herd was catching up on the sleds, passing – no longer driven, the dogs silent, the herders too. The entire caravan moved as one in the search for pasture, the need for shelter. Deer by deer, by twos, by threes, by tens and twenties, they flowed from behind, eyes fixed on their destination, and passed the sleds in a loping rhythm. They paid no earthly heed to their brothers, the transport-deer, clumsy and ugly in harness like a breed of slaves.

I stared back in awe into the dropping sun and saw them coming in their hundreds, thinned to a line by the banked snow above the track. They moved in a vast vapour of deer-breath and snow-spray.

As the sun grew molten they turned to silhouettes pouring through their own golden haze. Heads high and proud, their antlers swung from side to side in a swaying rhythm. The sun dropped lower. We crossed a ridge; the deer surged: light poured along a channel of branching horn, the untamed skulls of the bearers wild and proud, and the setting sunlight poured down along them in a river of gold as if the conjunction were precisely planned and they were meant to catch the sun in their chaliced antlers and hold it high against the Arctic night.

I looked at the transport-deer, dull shadows trooping beside my knees, heads blunt and low, shorn of horn but for some brute stumps missed by the saw. All their lives the beasts of burden are dragged against the earth. Their skulls are clamped in leather, shoulders pulled down by rawhide. They come down the blazing passes from beyond the sun, their gait unbearable, heroic.

SNAIL

Gréagóir Ó Dúill

Gréagóir Ó Dúill was born in Dublin and raised in Co. Antrim. He is executive director of the Poets' House, Falcarragh, Co. Donegal. Widely published as poet, editor, critic, short-story writer and biographer in Irish, his first collection in English is due from Lagan Press in spring 2005.

A large wall-map hung in our primary school. It was a political map in Mercator's projection and hung flat and one-dimensional out of our reach. So Canada was huge, Russia was threatening. It showed in detail what men made: cities, railways, frontiers. It accentuated the borders between nations, underlining them with sharp colour contrasts; empires had, each, their own colour. Antarctica was a pie divided into slices of different colours, of different sizes. We knew all about different sizes of slices of pie. Many names of large territories, painfully learnt, have since disappeared. Africa, in particular, I can no longer name; my colonisation was of short duration and the winds of change have blown away my labels.

But there was also, in school, a globe. It was large, made of tin, fixed at a strange angle to its axis. The teacher guarded it jealously but occasionally handed it over for exploration. The surface was not flat but ridged for mountains, gouged for rivers. There was little detail of what men made. Instead, the colours, greens, browns, blues and arctic white, marked the physical detail of the earth and the depth of the seas. We traced the Nile and danced the blue Danube, stubbed up against Tristan da Cunha, plumbed the depths of the Mindanao Trench. We felt the relationship of Calcutta to the Ganges and the Himalayas above. Our palm passed over Europe and met the sudden barrier of the Alps – an experience as vivid as when the cloud parted and my aeroplane window gave me a sudden view of peak and valley and glacier. This was geographic Braille, a tactile alphabet complementing the formal. It involved sight, as did reading and sums, but also touch, as did nothing else at school. The wall map showed theory and politics; the globe showed the situation on the ground. One did not last – when did I last say Bechuanaland, Pondicherri? The other taught lessons true and lasting and peaceful, serviceable to political change, the development of environmental theory, a bow to Gaia. It showed, as Mercator did not, true relative distances, the real size of the countries and seas; the globe did not distort.

Doubting Thomas insisted on research by fingertip and was allowed to proceed. Curiosity, the learning instinct, involves all five senses and involves, too, the teacher's readiness to hand over the fragile tin globe – trust and courage. At one stage of the long drawn out peace process I thought of a snail's decision to move, fraught as it is with dangers but with its own imperative. We covered the world with our small moving palms and filled our young minds. A snail covers so much less but does so with its whole body.

Shelled in for far too long, waiting the stamping foot:
Slow and cautious, with wavering antennae,
I smell and search
And move out slowly from my fortified base.
The slime of my trail shines silver,
The flower before me glows gold.
Life gallops past on its hobnails,
But the shell was too small,
Was no defence and in my stand I sank.
Afraid to move, I trembled, staying still
So cursed courageously
And bear my house on my shoulder as
I move into the day.
Eastwards from Dún Aengusa
Through the chevaux de frise
My black back swims shining in the light.
There are, yes, badgers, fangs, claws,
Beaks killing without cease,
But I, too, must eat and meet, to breed, to speak.

HOME

Cathal Ó Searcaigh

Cathal Ó Searcaigh lives at the foot of
Mount Errigal in Co. Donegal. The author
of ten poetry collections, his Irish language
poetry is widely translated and he has won
many awards including *The Irish Times* Prize
for Irish language literature. A member of
Aosdána, his latest book is *Seal in Neipeal*.

I became acutely aware of the word
'home' whilst I was cruising around
Piccadilly Circus, London, in the mid-
70s. 'A hustle here, a hustle there, hey
babe, take a walk on the wild side.' In
the camped-up lingo of Lou Reed I
was a thrill-seeking teenager, doing my
best to be self-indulgently hip. But I
was just a foppishly dressed yob from
the backcountry.

I felt uneasy being funky and, as a
result, I began to look into that terrible
dark pool of the self – *Dubheagán* as we

call it in Irish. At times like that, you realise you're an abyss, a pitch-black pit. There's only a deep darkness. You get dizzy looking down into the gulf, the chasm of yourself. You realise there's deafening silence. There are no answers. A poem became for me an act of defiance thrown in the face of that silence. I wrote poems of adolescent angst mostly. A poetry of pimples. I wrote bad poems because I didn't have the humility to read really good ones. Until one evening in the autumn of 1975 a man who worked in the storeroom of Oxford University Press walked into the pub where I worked and handed me a copy of Derek Mahon's latest collection, *The Snow Party*. That book had a profound effect on me, especially the first poem, called 'Afterlives'. Derek Mahon, a Belfast man, had gone to London at the beginning of the Northern troubles and I think he felt it on his conscience that he hadn't accounted for these terrible times in his poetry. So 'Afterlives' is a homecoming poem, in that Mahon came back to Belfast. The last verse was a real shock of recognition.

But the hills are still the same
Grey-blue above Belfast.
Perhaps if I'd stayed behind
And lived it bomb by bomb
I might have grown up at last
And learnt what is meant by home.

Home! The word just winged its way off the page. I felt the word as an intense desire to be reunited with something from which I felt I was cut off. The word was a smell from another world; the lost domain of my *Dúchas*. 'Dúchas' is a difficult word to explain in English, but briefly it means a sense of connection, a feeling of attachment to a place, a tongue and a tradition, a belief that one belongs to a sustaining cultural and communal energy; that one has a place and a name.

Suddenly I realised that I was in exile in an alien city where I neither had a face nor a name or a place. To be an exile meant to be on my own. It meant to be without the community's sense of warmth and settledness. I had to return home to reclaim my heritage, my *Dúchas*. And for me this *Dúchas* is not a flight into the past, rather a re-joining of the past, the present and the future. It is a quest, perhaps for an expanded present, which flows backwards and forwards with the one and same moment.

John Haines is an American poet and a true pioneer of the imagination. In 1947 he went to Alaska to homestead in the wilderness. There he discovered home and poetry.

I came to this place
A young man green and lonely

Well quit of the world
I framed a house with moss and timber
Called it a home
And sat in the warm evenings
Singing to myself as a man sings
When he knows there is
No-one to hear
I made my bed under the shadow
Of leaves and awoke
In the first snow of autumn,
Filled with silence.

Home! This word was a discovery but what is discovery only that which we remove the cover from. It has always been there – only hidden.

THE RIVER

Nuala Ní Chonchuir

Nuala Ní Chonchuir lives in Galway and has won the inaugural Cúirt New Writing Prize, the Francis Mac Manus Award and the Cecil Day Lewis Award. She has published one collection of poetry and, most recently, her first collection of short stories, *The Wind across the Grass*.

Reaching out from Wicklow's peat hags
and stretching into Poulaphouca,
she is home to eels, kingfishers
and the white bones of the dead.

Stacked one behind the other,
bridges grip her arm like bracelets
and her veins are the tea-brown spill
of the Tolka, the Poddle and the Wad.

Boats chase the length of her wrist
and plunge on past the Muglin Rocks,
pushing a path through mud and fish,
pointing their way out to sea.

When you grow up beside a river it becomes a part of who you are. You learn things about it without even realising; it's just a normal part of life. I was brought up in the Liffey Valley. Some people may think that the Liffey Valley is just a sprawling shopping centre, but in fact it is an area of outstanding natural beauty which stretches west into Kildare.

The house I grew up in looks over Glorney's Weir. The weir spans the river to the Strawberry Beds, a place that provided the Victorians with a day in the country without having to venture far from the city. The clock tower in the Farmleigh Estate lords it over the valley, the patina of its copper steeple blending with the trees that pack the slope below it.

As children, my sisters and brothers and I swam in the brown murk of the Liffey, avoiding jagged broken bottles and the deep pools that held rumours of drownings. We captured tadpoles and released them back into the shallows as frogs. We fished for eels there, taking them home to fry in butter, though I never actually went as far as tasting them. We built rafts of pallets and barrels and sailed and sank them. My uncle brought us over the quieter stretches in his green boat while we sang 'Row, row, row your boat' over and over again. In winter, when the river flooded the fields and then froze over, we skated on it. And at night the hush of the weir was like a lullaby, a comforting noise that was always there.

Of course we were warned of dangers and sometimes we got into trouble when a raft sank or fishing hooks got caught in our skin. But like most children who grew up in 1970s Ireland, we had freedom and we were left to explore the river and its banks as we chose.

I live on a housing estate in Galway now and I find that people are surprised when I say I'm from Dublin but that I was brought up surrounded by fields full of cows and horses, with a river running not fifty yards from the front door. Not for *my* sons the freedoms that I had. Their daily playground is a square of back garden and whatever expeditions we make as a family.

The beautiful Corrib River sneaks through the campus of the

university less than a mile from our house as it spills on towards the Atlantic Ocean. It's a comfort to have it so near to walk beside and to sail on and to show my sons all that a river can be. As the poet wrote:

> Empty indeed the childhood
> through which no river runs...

And while the river Corrib is truly lovely, it can never take the place of the Liffey, the river I grew up with, because I am a part of it and it's a part of me.

POOR SLOUGH

Rose Mary Logue

Rose Mary Logue is a chartered secretary and lives in Dublin. Ten years ago she gave up a full-time career in favour of a mixture of work, pottering in the garden, writing and having more time for friends.

John Betjeman bid friendly bombs fall on Slough. He considered:

> It isn't fit for humans now,
> There isn't grass to graze a cow!

Poor Slough.

Does anybody love the suburbs? Flick through glossy magazines and the homes you see featured are old Georgian houses surrounded by acres or ruined gate lodges, lovingly restored by persons with artistic leanings. You see penthouses in Temple Bar or bijou inner-city artisans' dwellings lauded and made to appear perfect as residences for those whose taste is impeccable. Rarely, if ever, will a three-bedroom semi be praised like that and they are often (I think rather disparagingly) referred to as 'starter homes', as if they can only be considered by those with insufficient money for anything better. And yet it is in such homes that the majority of city dwellers live. It is in such houses that those who have fuelled our economic boom were conceived and reared – in these houses poets, artists and writers have lodged.

Why are the suburbs often called soul-less? I don't know, because a soul certainly beats steadily in that part of South County Dublin where I live. This rich fertile land has been loved and tended from earliest times. The place names tell of Macud of Kilmacud, who accompanied St Brendan on his travels, Lorcan of Stillorgan, St Olave of Denmark who gave his name to Balally and St Nathi who left his monastery in Tallaght to seek seclusion in what was to be called Taney. This was the country of the O'Byrnes and O'Tooles, before the coming of the Normans. And the conquerors have also left their names here – Talbots, Pembrokes, Probys, Allens and Redesdales.

When I was a child, Dundrum, Stillorgan and Sandyford were still distinct villages. Granite walls, covered in ivy and valerian, bounded the roads and hedges of whitethorn, ash, sycamore and hazel divided the land. In the ditches grew cow parsley, primroses, violets, coltsfoot and horsetail. Each May the fields were awash with drifts of cowslips and dandelions. Little streams meandered along, populated by frogs and newts.

Between the villages the land was parcelled out around large houses, where lived gentlemen who commuted to Dublin on business. Some of the big houses were owned by religious orders, dedicated to the care of schools, orphans and the elderly. But whoever the occupants of these houses, in every case the surrounding land was farmed for the good food it produced – milk, beef, lamb and arable crops.

Many of the big houses remain, their uses changed with the

years. St Helen's on the Stillorgan Road was the novitiate of the Irish Christian Brothers in the 1950s. Now it is reborn as the Radisson Hotel. The novitiate of the Oblate Fathers at Galloping Green is today a home for the elderly. Several of the houses and farms were judiciously bought up by President Tierney of University College from the 1940s on. The old names are remembered on the campus – Thornfield, Woodview, Merville and Belfield House itself, which gave its name to the whole. Montrose has become synonymous with broadcasting. It was originally owned by UCD and swapped for Ardmore on the other side of the road.

Today almost the only representative of those dwelling houses with surrounding farmland is the Airfield Estate in Dundrum. Forty acres of level pasture and a large, but not grand, house, formerly owned by the Overend sisters, are now in the care of the Airfield Trust. Betjeman would have been pleased to know that here there is still grass to graze not one cow but several, together with sheep and poultry.

THE SOUND OF EXILE

Frank Corcoran

Frank Corcoran, composer, was born 1944 in pre-television Tipperary. The fair-day sounds of Borrisokane continue to reverberate through his cutting (Irish) edge works such as the mythic *Mad Sweeney* and *Quasi Una* orchestral series and his (own) funeral music for thirty-three pipers.

I'm an Irish exile living in the German city of Hamburg now for the best part of twenty years. Everyone says, 'What a lovely city.' I have a yen for what is not here in Hamburg, though. I notice it's not Irish. Never was. There are little subtle nuances in the different ways of going on that get under my Irish skin. Like what?

Well, I'm talking about differing ways of using language; I'll include body language, the twist of a phrase, irony, an ex-bilingualist's act of treachery in a tongue that's not his own. The local north Germans can tend to be literal minded in a mind-blowing way. 'The rat is on the mat'; let there be no nonsense or double meanings in talk. No mysteries, please, we're in Hamburg. We don't want any mystic guff about meaning behind meaning. As we say, 'Schnapps is schnapps and beer is beer.'

But the Irish know it's not that simple. What's that mystery behind the language you're using? One body language won't translate into another. Irish history won't translate either – it's too strange for the Hamburger to fathom. Translation is treachery. Anyway, Ireland NEVER features in German newspapers. Central European neighbours have more powerful pull – we look across the borders of Poland and Russia, down south across the Alps, to the west to France and, maybe, England. German tourists are delighted by Irish pub philosophers and our gift with some gab, our James Joyces. They've been pilgrims – witness Heinrich Böll's *Irish Journal* in left hand – in the land of black pints and magic gold butter from Kerry. It ends there, with at best half-successful efforts to interpenetrate the '*meon Gaelach*', '*die irische Mentalität*', the conundrums of our cultural history. Yes, the national German poet, Mr Goethe, was enthralled in the 1790s by MacPherson's Edinburgh Ossianic forgeries of the Fianna Cycle of stories. A certain German composer living in Vienna was, I'm delighted to say, sent across twelve Irish airs to set for the then music market. Beethoven possessed little English, less Gaeilge. He did a good job with his *Irish Lieder*. The cheque for commissioning fee was sent over via a Hamburg bank. His musical settings are a monstrosity. There's no '*nea*' – how could there be? How could this lack of contact between two very different histories lead to a spark of insight into what we Irish have been up to these last few hundred years is what I ask myself – daily, hourly – in this bracing, north German climate.

I treasure the few valuable links I run across. There were precious few between eighteenth-century Gaelic Ireland and eighteenth-century Hanseatic Hamburg. One of the strangest concerns that strange slow air, 'Tadhg Buí', 'red-haired Tadhg'. Tadhg, the red-haired poet and musician, died in the year of our Lord 1787, a long way from Tipperary, in Hamburg. The words to this magnificent tune paint the poet: *'Más Tadhg buí mé, tá croí agam níos gile ná cailc'* – 'I'm Tadhg Buí, but I've a heart whiter than chalk/It is with a grand high style I'd write every letter properly.' What were the letters this eighteenth-century exile from Munster wrote on his wanderings through Europe? We will never know. Maybe one line of this Hamburg-Ireland linked slow air gives me a clue: *'Fóiríor bhocht!'* – 'For the likes of me, the drink is the danger.'

OK, a few tourists will have come across Roger Casement's visit to the Kaiser in Berlin in 1916 and the submarine delivery of all those rusty Mauser rifles on lonely Banna Strand but it stops there. You'd need a lot of interaction in politics and sport and arts and youth exchange and God-knows-what to improve the inter-rubbing of two radically different ways to manufacture spectacles; to see reality. I feel this daily here in exile: the different ways the Celtic and the Teutonic tribes utter inhabiting this world. These two worlds is what I'm trying to say. Take an average Hamburger's reaction to my singing a bit of a tune on his spotlessly swept street. Or I chance a, 'Grand day today, thank God!'

Translation is treachery.

THE HIGHEST
PLACE ON
EARTH

Pat Falvey

Pat Falvey, adventurer, explorer and
motivational speaker, has led over thirty-
eight successful expeditions to some of the
coldest, highest and loneliest places worldwide. He has lived with tribes on several
continents, studying the traits of mankind.

This was it. The last few metres to
the highest place on earth. I was
now about to cross the highest
platform on earth. There were
thousands of feet of fall-off on all
sides, as I walked on this narrow ridge
with the world below my feet.

A feeling of excitement rose from
the pit of my stomach to fill my
heaving chest. Approaching the last fifty
metres, my emotions were running riot.
Those few minutes were the most
amazing moments of my life. Step by

step by lingering step, I inched my way to the top, stopping every few steps for a rest and taking in one of the greatest views on earth.

With about fifty metres to go something very strange happened to me. I began to feel as if my soul and body had somehow parted company. It was as if I was having an out-of-body experience: my soul was hovering a few hundred feet above me as it watched my mortal body, which was under severe pressure due to fatigue, slowly making its way to the pinnacle ahead. Unsure whether I was alive or dead I continued, like a moth attracted to the light of a candle, to the summit ahead.

Tears of joy streamed from my eyes and froze on my beard as the awesome Himalayan chain started to unfold below.

Glaciers, which, for hundreds of thousands of years, have been slipping down the sides of these enormous rock formations, lay spread out on all sides like fingers on the welcoming hand of the mountain.

I will never forget the last few steps, and there I was, standing on top of the world. I could have roared with joy but instead I silently prayed. Thoughts of those who had gone before me, and those who sadly never completed the journey back to Base Camp, ran through my mind.

My partners, James and Mike, and I just stood there in silence for a minute and then turned 360 degrees to take in the greatest view on this earth. I was conscious that this was not just another climbing exploit. After many years of dreaming, planning, fund-raising, fretting, risk-taking – and, on occasion, being more single-minded than was fair to those close to me – I had stepped from dreamland into the bright, sharp light of reality.

It was quiet and peaceful as we stood on that patch of sacred ground, six miles high in the sky. There were no television cameras, no press and no roaring crowds to distract me. The time we spent there was very beautiful and gave me a personal, inner satisfaction that was calming and private. I was excited and elated beyond description. I was so proud to be an Irishman standing on the summit of the Goddess Mother of the Earth – Mt Everest

FOOD AND NATIONALITY

Paolo Tullio

Paolo Tullio is a restaurant reviewer, writer, actor and broadcaster, whose credits include the television series and book *North of Naples, South of Rome, mushroom.man* — a novel set on the Internet — and parts in *The Butcher Boy, The General* and, most recently, *The Tailor of Panama.*

Perhaps the biggest difference between the Irish and the Italians is their attitude to food. In the almost entirely secular state of Italy, food is the nearest thing to a religion. It's as commonly part of conversation as the weather is here. It's all-pervasive, it's all-consuming but most of all it's very good.

Much of the time spent during the day is devoted to food, not just preparing it but also buying it. Watch an Italian woman buying fruit. She won't even contemplate picking up a ready-made bag with a kilo of oranges in it. She'll pick up oranges from a pile, one at a time, squeeze each one, check for blemishes and slowly put together her choice. This is repeated for all the vegetables that she needs. Everything is examined minutely; only produce that fits her exacting standards will be bought. Time spent in selection is not considered time wasted; it is important to ensure that food quality is of the finest possible.

Huge bakeries with fleets of vans supplying bread for a fifty-mile radius are unheard of. Even tiny villages have their own bakery so that fresh bread can be bought twice a day. Italian bread has the same property as French bread, it goes hard quickly, so supplies are bought little and often. Despite the fact that there is a bakery in every village, people still travel to find the best bread. There is a bakery in the next town to mine known as Cessinella which has a permanent queue. People from villages at the other end of valley come here to buy bread and pizza, passing four or five bakeries on the way. Quality is appreciated and no effort is too much to seek it out.

Living in Ireland, where fish is plentiful, cheap and almost completely unappreciated, I find the Italian attitude to fish remarkable. In Italy fish is a treat, a special food for special occasions, and not a penance for Fridays. It is also expensive; a meal in a restaurant will double in price when fish is served. For an honoured guest at dinner the menu will certainly contain fish, or will be entirely composed of it. Again, time and trouble are no obstacle when it comes to obtaining it. Although it can be bought frozen in supermarkets or fresh in the markets, it is not unusual for people in our valley to drive to Formia or Gaeta, an eighty-mile round trip, to buy their fish at the quayside. Nobody considers this exceptional or extreme behaviour. How else can you be sure the fish is as fresh as possible?

What it all comes down to is that Italians believe food is important. Its supply and preparation forms a large part of their day. They really believe that quality in the ingredients is paramount, and they'll spare no effort to ensure they get the best. And when you think about it, it makes sense. Food is the one sensory pleasure that can be enjoyed several times a day, right up to the day of our demise.

DOGO ONSEN

Mary Arrigan

Mary Arrigan, award-winning author/
illustrator, was born in Newbridge, Co.
Kildare, and now lives in Roscrea, Co.
Tipperary. As well as teenage fiction, she
writes and illustrates books for younger
children. Her books have been translated
into seven languages.

Shikoku Island off the south coast
of Japan is reached by train across
the expansive Seto-ohashi Bridge. Its
biggest city, Matsuyama, has an ancient
atmosphere that marks it out from
most of the other post-bombing
reconstructed cities of Japan. It's a
shock to arrive and find that all the
signs are in Japanese — which makes it
a bit of a pantomime trying to find a
hotel, since nobody speaks English
either. Accosting people by closing
your eyes and making snoring noises in

an effort to find out where you can sleep can make you feel a right nellie.

One of the highlights of Matsuyama is the Dogo Onsen – the ancient spa bathhouse. Entry to this is very confusing, especially when you can't read. One door takes you to a locker room where you leave your shoes. Another door takes you to the front where you're given a yakuta (dressing gown). Then it's on to the changing rooms and, finally, the bathhouse. Get the sequence of exits and entrances wrong and you flounder – just like I did. After parting with my shoes, I wandered straight to the changing rooms. It didn't strike me as strange then that I had neither dressing gown nor towel.

The female bathhouse was a huge circular affair, with an oriental stone creature spouting the steaming spa water from his fanged mouth. Around the wall were low stools set in front of miniature showers. I gathered the idea was to have a scrub before entering the communal bath. So scrub I did. Not well enough, it seemed. I was set upon by a small naked old lady who wagged her hairy chin at me and screeched, '*Gaijin* [foreigner]! You wash!' OK. Maybe she had noticed I missed a bit, so I sat down and washed again until all my wobbly bits glowed. Like some sort of oriental reverend mother, the old lady was upon me again. This time she thrust a wooden bucket into my hand, poked me with a knobbly finger and screeched again, '*Gaijin! Gaijin!* You wash!'

Standing white and bare in a roomful of sepia-coloured female bodies and being yelled at is a very solitary thing. Perhaps I should have just gone to some temple.

'I have washed,' I protested.

But the whiskery chin was on overdrive now. '*Gaijin!* Wash!' I looked at the bucket, wondered what I was supposed to do with it, handed it back and, dirty foreigner or not, got into the pool. Nobody died. It was later, when I went back to the dressing room and found myself without towel or yakuta, that I realised I had come in the wrong way. That meant dressing without drying and finding the proper entrance to get the towel and dressing gown. A polite lady, with the aid of sketches on the condensation, directed me.

Wrong door – men's dressing room. I should really have gone to that temple. I finally got my yakuta, hung my wet clothes to dry and went up to the veranda where green tea and dainty biscuits were served to me on my own reserved mat – a pleasure cut short when a familiar whiskery chin loomed into view. It was very gratifying to see that her feet were dirty.

PHOTOGRAPH

Patrick Treacy

Dr Patrick Treacy is Medical Director of the
Ailesbury Clinic (Ireland) and of Therapie
and the Body Clinics (UK and Ireland) and
is recognised as Ireland's leading cosmetic
doctor. He has travelled throughout dozens
of countries and is editor of *Treacy's Tales*,
www.treacystales.com

The air was still and hot and it
hung close like a damp cloth over
the Australian desert scrubland. I arose
and walked out to the wooden patio to
watch the early sunrise, a smouldering
cauldron of crimsons and pinks that
almost seemed to set fire to the distant
horizon. There was always magic in the
wakening morn, as the noises and
colours of the sandy orange environment began to change and morning
spilled a bucket of orange paint across
the plains and washed away the purple

hues of night. It was indeed a magnificent morning to be alive in the outback, amidst this swirling canvas of fiery colour that announced the coming of another day.

For a while I stared out at the beauty and wildness of the arid landscape, watching as an old Aboriginal woman approached along the dirt track that snaked through the town. She walked with slow shuffling steps, dragging oversized shoes through the red murram dust, which rose in plumes about her. It settled on her green shawl and kilted clothing, coating her unkempt hair and rounded face, filling in each craggy line to make her look younger than her many years. She came from the local Barkindji tribe, a clan supposedly charged with the custodianship of the land and all living things upon it. Her people lived in a collection of dirty tin shacks that nestled around the Darling riverbank, a sleepy place where children ran naked along the paprika sand and lethargic dogs stretched and scratched under the shade of the Coolabah trees.

For a while I watched her getting closer and noted how her graceless movements appeared to be in total contrast with the rest of the emergent dawn. It was almost as if some divine being still had some unfinished work to do here in the barren outback. She carried a small stick, possibly to poke for roots or even catch one of those lizards with the whippish tongues that darted across the desert floor. Eventually she stopped beneath my patio and began looking at some old stones that littered the edge of the roadside. The sun had started on its journey from the horizon and the morning light fell about the dry, yellow grass and threw shadows on some markings on the stones that I hadn't noticed before. I watched her as she cupped her jaw in her left hand and began alternately looking attentively into the pattern and then at me. I went back into the bedroom to get my camera. A small breeze got up and, for a while, we watched each other through the conduit of a camera lens before those unwavering tea-bag eyes looked deep inside and I got embarrassed and turned away. They whispered to me and told me tales about her dead forefathers and her people's lost dignity.

The irreverent cackle of a blue winged kookaburra called out from a nearby tree, insensitive to the old woman's moment of spiritual retreat, as all around us daylight noises began to merge into the other sounds of the new dawn. Then she got up and left, wandering further out into the bush, turning every now and then as if the scrubland came complete with traffic lights and road signs. In the distance I watched as she disappeared, swallowed by the desert landscape and the shadows that fell fast upon the morn.

THOUGHTS IN A KENYAN CEMETERY

Martin Ryan

Martin Ryan is a scriptwriter and biographer. His *William Francis Butler: A Life,
1838–1910* was published by the Lilliput
Press in 2003. His radio work includes
portraits of Karen Blixen and Franz Liszt.

Just south of the equator, almost six
thousand feet up the western slopes
of Mount Kenya, sprawls the town of
Nyeri. This is Kikuyu country: green,
hilly, well watered and fertile. The land
is heavily populated and Nyeri itself,
the raucous commercial capital of
Kenya's Central Province, is
clangourous. But the town has pockets
of stillness and one of these is its small
Anglican cemetery.

The cemetery's perimeter hedging
is ragged and straggly, its grass and

walkways are in need of some maintenance and its graves are a mix of the well tended and the overgrown. Laid out on the edge of a ridge, it gives a sweeping view across to the jagged summit of Mount Kenya. This snow-tipped mountain, rising almost seventeen thousand feet above sea level, is the home of God, or Ngai, in Kikuyu tradition. From here the creator looks at the world below and watches the strivings and vanities of mortals.

To read your way through the headstones in the cemetery is to touch something of the diversity of recent Kenyan history. Take this, for example:

In loving memory of our dear father Daniel Weru Riitho
Who died on 13th November 1968 aged about 120 years

It's that phrase, 'about 120 years', that startles. Before the coming of colonialism, a Kikuyu's actual year of birth was not formally marked. Instead, a child joined an age band. In the case of Daniel Weru, even allowing for exaggeration — after all, who lives to 120 years? — his century-plus of life encompassed the entire colonial period in Kenya. As a young man he saw the arrival of European rule. As an old man he saw its departure.

The largest plot in the cemetery has a sharper reminder of colonial times. It holds about thirty graves.

Private George Chapman. Died 1955 age 19
At the going down of the sun
We shall remember him

2nd Lieutenant A.G. Warnes. Died 1954 age 19
So dearly loved. So sadly missed

Private G.R. Crowde. Died 1953 age 18

And so on. Those are some of the young men killed during what was once known as the Mau Mau Rebellion and is now known as the Kenyan Independence Struggle. Most of them had grown up in Kenya; their parents had come out as settlers and administrators in the early part of the twentieth century, never envisaging just how short their idyll in this beautiful country would be. That first generation is also remembered in this cemetery.

Many of them lived long lives, but fevers and accidents brought others to early graves. One of these was Heben Carpenter. The inscription on his crude headstone is spare but pithy:

Heben Carpenter of Okehampton, Devon.
Born 3rd Dec 1901
Killed by a Rhino 14th Jan 1936

The names of some of those laid to rest at Nyeri still strike a faint cord for today's world. Big Jim Corbett, the Indian-born tiger hunter, is buried here. So are the missionaries Mary and Grey Leakey, whose son Louis almost single-handedly was to bring African paleo-anthropology to world attention. But most visitors who stop off here with a purpose come to view one particular grave: the final resting-place of Robert Baden-Powell, the founder of the boy scouts – the most widespread, sustained and successful of twentieth-century youth movements.

Baden-Powell's remains lie in a double grave with those of his wife Olave, who led the Girl Guide movement for many years. In old age, ill health brought him to Nyeri for recuperation and he spent the last few years of his life here. The focal point of his simple off-white marble headstone is a black circle cut into the stone. At the centre of the circle is a heavy black dot. This is the scouting trail sign which means *I have gone home*. It could not be more apt. The sign faces the glinting glaciated peaks of God's mountain, symbolising the spiritual element of life, while in the grave over which it stands, mortal remains slowly decompose in Nyeri's fertile red earth.

SAN JUAN CHAMULA

Marguerite MacCurtain

Marguerite MacCurtain is a travel writer and broadcaster.

The village of San Juan Chamula nestles in an alpine-type setting, twelve kilometres north-east of the city of San Cristobal in Mexico. The Chamula Indians are an indigenous group whose history is steeped in blood, repression and exploitation from colonial times to the present day. As a consequence, they are suspicious of strangers and, on occasion, have been known to be very hostile towards tourists. Religion plays a central part in the life of the Chamula people.

They acknowledge St John the Baptist as the main god of their universe and Jesus Christ as his younger brother, and they once crucified a boy so that they would have their own Christ.

A journey to San Juan Chamula is fraught with other dangers for the visitor because the Chiapas region where it is situated is politically very volatile. But if the political climate is stable, it is possible to walk through the valleys to this legendary village and it was at such a moment that I made that journey with my friend, Heather, a few years ago.

We walked over dusty, ochre-coloured paths where women dressed in local costume and washed clothes in the streams, while children laughed and played in the early morning sunshine. Red roofs peeped out from amongst the forest clearings of the surrounding hillsides. Vendors were dotted along the way, selling locally woven textiles and rainbow-coloured jewellery from their stalls. Everyone greeted us in a warm and friendly way and we arrived without incident in the village square.

We bought our permits at the Tourist Centre and walked through the white, horseshoe-shaped archway towards the church door. Here the guardian, a small man dressed in traditional rough wool trousers and tunic with a wide brimmed hat and armed with a long stick like a shillelagh, was waiting for us.

He took our permits and scrutinised them for what seemed to be a long time. Then he scrutinised each of us from head to toe. His eyes fixed on Heather's camera. After a considerable pause he beckoned me to enter but barred my friend by blocking her way with his big stick. When she protested he chased her from the church grounds furiously, waving the stick and shouting at her. When I gestured that I would also leave, he chased me inside and closed the door. Then he calmly sat back into his chair. I decided to stay put for fear of antagonising him again.

The interior of the church consisted of a central nave and apse. There were no side aisles or pews. The floor was tiled in green and blue tiles and was sprinkled with pine needles. Figureless wooden crosses wrapped in white satin were stacked against the walls amongst fragrant branches of strongly scented pine. Flowers and candles were set before saints dressed in Spanish capes, silver paper crowns and mirror pendants. These were the saints currently in favour. Those out of favour were broken into a pile at the end of the church. The thorn-crowned figure of Christ lay in a casket in the apse out of sight.

A group of perhaps a dozen people and a baby sat in a circle around an arrangement of offerings, about half-way up the nave towards the left-hand side. A male from the family invited me to sit with them. The baby slept while the family prayed and recited incantations. A selection of foodstuffs and drinks, including eggs, grain, maize, sugar, chocolate, Coca-Cola, water and beer, were grouped in neat rows before an arrangement of candles. I counted ninety-nine candles in all grouped in numbers of twelve and fourteen around one large candle. All were lit. I was offered Coca-Cola and beer to drink and chocolate to eat. The praying and incantations continued. Grain, sugar, maize, Coca-Cola and beer were sprinkled over the baby at intervals. The eggs were moved closer to the baby then waved in the air around the child several times before being carried from the church by a male member of the family. I learned later that the purpose of this ceremony is to transfer the illness to the eggs and then smash them at a distance from the church. The belief is that the child or person will then be restored to full health.

When I got up to leave the males stood up, each one taking my hand in both of his and speaking gently a few words that I did not understand. The women smiled. I approached the guardian nervously. He stood up, smiled and opened the church door. I walked out into the hot sunshine of the afternoon and rejoined my friend Heather. We began our journey back to the city of San Cristobal. In distance it was twelve kilometres. In reality I felt it was an eternity away from the people of San Juan Chamula.

HOLIDAYS

Kate Thompson

Kate Thompson is a best-selling novelist, whose most recent publication is *Living the Dream*. Her next — *Sex, Lies & Fairytales* — is due in 2005. All her novels have been widely translated.

My mother loved to remind me of an incident from my childhood. As she passed the bathroom door one evening, she heard me talking to myself. I was, most likely, soaking in a bubble bath, picturing myself in some 'Hollywood starlet' scenario, because the sentiment that was being given utterance from behind the bathroom door went thus: *Money ... to buy ... champagne.* I have always hankered after luxury, and I'm convinced that it's because, as a child, my parents used to take us on camping holidays. Not the kind of camping holidays that are commonplace today, you understand – the kind of holiday where you pitch your tent in a site with 'facilities' such as showers and laundries and restaurants and shops. Oh, no. Our camping holidays would have made the Royal Marines look like My Little Pony Camp. Our tents were ex-army, as were our camp beds. My mother heated up tins of dubious stew over a Primus stove and gathered water from rivers. When you saw a family member heading into a thicket with a spade and a pained expression, you just – *didn't ask*. My father despised namby-pambyism. When he sent me and my brother off in the rain to chase after lambs up Mount Errigal, instructing us to bring one home for dinner, we didn't realise he was joking. We really feared for those lambs.

Each time we went away on one of our so-called 'holidays', one of my chores was to go to the local farm with a jerry can for milk. So was it any wonder, as I grew up and all my friends started going on exotic holidays to places like Tenerife, that I hankered after 'money to buy champagne' and fantasised about talcum-powder beaches and palm trees and sun loungers? There appeared to be only one job option open to me that would earn me enough money to finance my perfect holiday, so I joined Trinity Players and set about becoming a film star.

Later, when the man who became my husband and I were struggling actors, *any* holiday was a rare luxury. Ironic, because when you're (to use that fey thespian term) 'resting' you have all the time in the world to take off on holiday, but never enough money to go anywhere exotic.

We did get to head to the West Coast of Ireland a lot – my mother-in-law has a mobile home in a glorious situation overlooking Clew Bay – but that never seemed like a *proper* holiday. We still had to cook and clean and keep an eye on our daughter Clara and the hordes of friends who would join her – and the mobile home is hardly the last word in luxury. It's been there for thirty years now and has what might euphemistically be described as a 'lived-in look'. While beauty board, swirly acrylic carpets and

FOOD FROM THE WILD

Gerry Galvin

Gerry Galvin, retired restaurateur and chef, is the author of several best-selling cookbooks and a published poet and magazine columnist. His first novel is nearing completion and he lives in Moycullen, Co. Galway.

Salad, on restaurant menus these days, is often described mundanely as mixed leaves, indicating the use of different lettuces, sometimes with the addition of edible herbs which are usually cultivated in commercial greenhouses or, in some cases, actually gathered from the wild. Foraging for wild foods has ceased to be viewed as a dangerous eccentricity, and it is a measure of serious cooking to feature *cuisine sauvage*, as the French call it. I have been a promoter of wild food since the 1970s, when Hedli McNeice, the then doyenne of Kinsale restaurateurs, introduced me to sea beet, also called sea spinach, which she collected on a patch of waste ground adjoining the sea near the Old Head of Kinsale. Sea beet thrives throughout the summer around the Irish coast, close to beaches, on sea walls and on paths. It is a firmer and stronger plant than its various cultivated relatives, but its taste is much the same as garden spinach, and it is, of course, full of valuable iron and minerals.

It was in West Cork also that I first found fennel, fronds of it waving in the sea breeze, protected by a roadside wall near Timoleague. There is no more aggressive herb, growing profusely in exotic plumes of hair-like leaves. Its scent is strongly of aniseed, which is much prized in fish cookery.

I have been using wild herbs for years. Ubiquitous stinging nettles are old friends and, like constant friends, sometimes unfairly maligned – a case of familiarity breeding contempt! Nettles were a subsistence food during the Famine in the 1840s. Nettle soup spiced with nutmeg, using potatoes as a thickener, is tempting on any menu. A free-range egg on a base of nettle purée, baked with a scattering of grated cheese, is a healthy and attractive-looking dish. All you need for harvesting nettles are gloves, a pair of scissors and a bucket. According to a nineteenth-century family herbal guide, nettles 'taken inwardly in moderate quantity' were capable of exciting the system and acting as an aphrodisiac. For really assiduous lovers, a few oysters added to a bowl of nettle soup should work wonders for the libido. A note of caution: nettles cooked after the end of May are excessively laxative. And therein's the sting!

You can make soups with watercress, always mindful that the cooking kills off the liver-fluke larvae which can be transmitted from sheep and cattle to humans. The simple, effective rule is always to cook wild watercress before you eat it.

Walking through many damp woodlands, anytime from the

end of March into May, one is almost certain to become aware of a pervasive smell of garlic. The source is ramsons, or wild garlic, which grows with aromatic abandon in Ireland. The leaves are bright green and the beautiful flowers, with delicate snow-white petals, are a startling contrast to the dark green of the woods. They are a wonderful food source as soups or blended into sauces. They give a distinctive tang to salads, and you can make delicious garlic butter by mixing chopped leaves with softened butter. I wrote a Haiku once, which went like this:

In the wood a soup
Anticipating springtime
Damp, garlicky green.

LYON

Éamonn Ó Catháin

Éamonn Ó Catháin was born in Belfast and
started eating shortly thereafter, only paus-
ing to collect records. These days, he can
been seen on his TV series for TG4, *Bia's
Bothar*, and heard on RTÉ Radio I, BBC
Radio Ulster and Raidió na Gaeltachta.
His latest book is *Around Ireland with a Pan*.

I recently made what must be my tenth
visit to Lyon, in France. It's a lovely
city and I went there the first time
because it grandly offers itself to be the
Capital of Gastronomy in the World.
I'm no longer taken in by that, but I
find it a handsome city and return there
when I can for the many things that it
offers – a delightful Roman amphi-
theatre, lovely walks, charming and
remarkable vineyards to the north and
south of the city, cheap and cheerful
food and its three rivers – the Saône,
the Rhone and the Beaujolais.

When I first went there I was lucky enough to find what became my favourite restaurant in the whole world – La Tour Rose. It's in the heart of the old city, and I have been fortunate enough to dine there maybe five times. These days, though, it's very much out of my pocket, and so I just gaze wistfully in the door and at the menu, largely unchanged since 1986. I content myself with eating in its sister bistro, Le Comptoir du Boeuf just across the road, at one tenth of the price. Old Lyon needs to be approached with a lot of trepidation – it's a tourist trap but a delightful one, full of cobbles and *traboules* (of which more anon), impossibly high stairways up the side of the hill and puppet and delf museums, all dominated by the fabulous basilica on the hill – Fourviere. Every time I climb up to it, forsaking the funicular, I read about its history and origin and the story of its construction, and every time I make the tortuous descent on the Way of the Rosary I forget. But it is beautiful, and there is a magnificent vista of the second city of France from its grounds.

But that word *traboule*: it is one of a number of words unique to the Lyonnais, some of which have passed into modern French and are used throughout the hexagon of France without those speakers knowing where they have come from. The *traboules* are the alleyways, which crisscross Lyon, many of which were used first by the silk-weavers whose industry supported the city and later the resistance in their heroic stand against the Nazis who wreaked untold havoc on the city. It has given rise to a verb, '*trabouler*', which means to walk aimlessly around the *traboules*, many of which now shelter shops, little restaurants or informal cafes. The other word in Lyon is the ubiquitous '*pot*'; these days everyone in France will say '*on va prendre un pot*', the exact equivalent of our 'ya coming for a jar', but the actual pot itself remains uniquely Lyonnais. It is a special wine bottle which holds neither 37.5 cl nor 75 cl but a spot-on 46 cl. I say spot-on because it is the perfect measure, just right for an individual, an admirable size to grace any table. Gone forever the ceaseless arguments about white or red: one can just order a pot of both. These pots are to be found in the city's eating places which are called '*bouchons*'; neither café nor restaurant, they are a mixture of both and are the city's inns. They have great big barrels of southern Beaujolais and northern Rhone wines and, of course, the city's own favourite: the Coteaux du Lyonnais, quaffed lovingly by working-men and silk-weaving women city-wide. Poured without ceremony straight from the barrel and into the pot, they will leave you wanting more, for such is their fruitiness and drinkability. Their slight price will leave you able to afford more.

Don't expect to get a steak though; the city thrives on innards and gizzards and entrails and tripe and pike and whatever is fresh at the market that day. Fast food may exist side-by-side with the *bouchons*, but international cuisine has never made its mark on the city's. Whatever you eat, though, don't miss out on two things. First is the city's remarkable cheese, St Marcellin; you are usually served an entire individual one, not a sliver, with bread, not crackers, and a walnut salad. It is truly delicious and rarely seen outside its native city. The other is a cheese concoction in honour of the city's former work-force and called *cervelle de canut* or 'silkweavers' brains'. *Canut* was the name given to the silk-weavers who were an all-important part of Lyon's population and economy; *cervelle* or brains is no more than a reference to the appearance of the dish – it is also called *claquaret* because the cheese (which should be 'male' or firm) has been well-beaten or *claque*. Every restaurant makes it fresh with fromage blanc, shallots, parsley, chervil and chives, white wine and white wine vinegar, sometimes pink peppercorns, and serves it between the main course and dessert without so much as a by-your-leave. Everyone eats it. Make sure you do.

SWIMMING
ROUND THE
ISLAND

Alannah Hopkin

Alannah Hopkin has published two novels
and various stories. As an arts journalist
she works mainly for the *Irish Examiner, The
Irish Times* and *The Sunday Tribune*. She lives
in Kinsale.

We are lucky in Kinsale because
we have an ideal swimming
place, Sandy Cove. There is a channel
about 300 yards across between the
mainland and a small island,
uninhabited apart from a flock of wild
goats. We swim across to the island
and back and every so often there is an
organised swim, with rescue boats and
proper safety precautions, around the
island.

The swimming season starts in
June. The first swim of the year is cold

enough to hurt, but the trick is not to give up, to swim through the pain barrier. One of the great pleasures of sea swimming is that all you need is a comfortable swimsuit, a rubber hat and a pair of goggles. Only wimps swim in wet suits.

I first swam around the island, a distance of a mile and a bit, on a calm August evening two years ago. I was apprehensive because I do not swim the crawl, I swim breaststroke slowly. I am what serious, head-down swimmers call 'a sightseer' – I like to look at the scenery and the wildlife as I swim. It takes me about forty-five minutes to swim a mile compared to about twenty minutes for a fast swimmer. But I love it.

You push off from the quay along with the rest of the slow group, maybe ten other swimmers, and head out around the western end of the island to the open sea.

There is a wonderful moment as you pass the tip of the island, when all you can see up ahead is sea, sea as far as the horizon. You forget about the other swimmers, the spectators, the rescue boats, your husband on the point with binoculars, your sister on the quay worrying; everything goes. There is just you and the sea. It is at once the loneliest and the most exciting feeling – there is just you, a small insignificant mammal, two arms and two legs working away, and this vast, black sea. What am I doing here? The scale is awesome.

Going down the outside of the island is quite different from swimming in its shelter. The surge is much stronger, but not unpleasant. On a big, organised swim, we disturb the nesting gulls who fly overhead in great shrieking flocks.

The first time around you learn a cruel fact; the east end of the island is not a point like its west end, but it is another side. The island is a triangle, not an oval, as it appears from land. But the views are good and you know there is sheltered water waiting around the corner.

Back in the inner harbour there is still about fifteen minutes to go. By now I have caught my third wind, a great moment, when you know for sure that you can keep on until you are back at the quay, and hardly a feather out of you. Maybe it's adrenaline or the famous endorphin high – whatever it is, it's nice.

And then, when you come to the slip and you are among the last home, still swimming your leisurely breaststroke, which has become automatic like a reflex action by this stage, the kindly spectators give you a big cheer as you get out of the water and stand on dry land again and you feel, just for a nanosecond, like a hero. Your muscles are toned and stretched, your heartbeat is low and steady, you feel good, very good. Within seconds you are shivering uncontrollably, teeth chattering loudly, but it was great and you'd do it again any time. 'Honestly, it was great, I enjoyed it,' you keep saying and the non-swimmers shake their heads in disbelief.

NIAGARA FALLS

Peter Philips

Peter Philips' first book was *Humanity Dick*, the biography of Richard Martin, followed by *The Great German Escape*. He is currently working on a book and TV documentary looking at the Fenian invasions of Canada.

It is difficult to understand the magnitude of Niagara Falls. The words 'awesome' and 'natural wonder' are often overused, but here they can be applied together. Anybody that has been there will confirm that after about three hours you will have seen the Falls from the American side, the Canadian side, from a boat, from a cave behind the water and from the tall spiky building on top of the casino.

Now, if you have ventured there on a day trip from Toronto or New York, that's fine, because you go back having seen just about enough spectacle. If, however, you are committed to be there for any longer period of time, you now have a problem.

This is why a tourist industry of

secondary attractions has built up. If I tell you that one of the major attractions is the Rock 'n' Roll Waxworks, and their window display consists of two identical tailor's dummies – one adorned with a black wig, heavy eye make-up and a snake; the other a blond wig, large glasses and platform boots – you will probably have got a handle on the quality and depth of Niagara's tourist infrastructure.

Worry not. Half an hour's drive away is the scene of one of the most amazing, bizarre and little heard of events in Irish history.

I first came across it doing some research for a book set in the middle of the nineteenth century. When looking at a summary of the events of 1866, I read, virtually as a throw-away fact, that the year also saw the Irish military invasion of Canada.

After staring at the page for a while, I dropped what I was doing, compelled to immediately look into this in more detail. And it is true. More to the point, very few people seem to have heard about it, and those that do have bought the generally delivered version that it was a minor event and can be summed up as a shambolic raid of no historic significance. Not so.

Having now researched and written about this extraordinary page of Irish history, let me share some of the highlights.

During the American Civil War, tens of thousands of Irishmen had bravely fought for the union. With the war over, those who had survived were battle-hardened, experienced soldiers and also out of work.

Meanwhile, the Fenian movement was probably at its peak in America, with its own senate, backed by a well-organised fund-raising machine. They considered themselves a government in exile. What they needed, however, was a plan to bring the British government to its knees, leading to their goal of independence for Ireland. They had concluded that bombing the occasional police station was not going to achieve this.

At face value, the British military might would always succeed. However, when the wider picture is looked at, there were vulnerabilities. Britain was stretched around the world. Mutinies and wars in India and China had not been completely dealt with, and decades of conflict had left the British treasury empty. A threat was also emerging from Prussia. Britain had one thing going for her: she still possessed the mightiest navy in the world. Where better to attack her than 1,500 miles from the sea?

A plan was conceived. An army of 30,000 men would be recruited in America. Two-thirds would assemble along Lake Erie and invade Canada. The British troops dispatched from Toronto, and reinforced from Montreal, would be easily defeated. This would allow a third Fenian regiment to invade across the Canadian border from Vermont, where the unprotected St Lawrence River would be secured, preventing any British reinforcements from arriving by sea. Britain would have no choice but to grant Ireland independence in return for her North American property. The alternative was for the Fenian senate to establish an overseas Irish Republic in what are now Ontario and Quebec.

General Tom 'Fightin' Sweeney, one of the most decorated soldiers in the Union Army, and an Irish man to boot, was recruited to mastermind the operation, and on 1 June 1866 the plan swung into action.

Looking back, it is difficult to see how it could go wrong, but wrong it went. However, not before the spearhead troops invaded across the Niagara River from Buffalo, New York. Near the small town of Ridgeway they engaged the British Army and won the resulting battle. This remains the only time an Irish army has inflicted a defeat on the British outside of Ireland and raised the tricolour on British territory. It is, in fact, the only time Ireland has ever invaded another country.

And it is all there to see. Twenty miles down the road from Niagara Falls is the little town of Ridgeway. It has a wonderful museum and the original building, which was used as a field hospital, has been converted into a heritage centre. If you go there, buy a booklet written by David Owen, a local historian. It will give you a fascinating tour of the area, highlighting all the events surrounding the invasion. Even if military history is not your cup of tea, you get to see some great views across the river to Buffalo.

Trust me, it's far more interesting than the Rock 'n' Roll Waxworks.

THE FASTNET
LIGHTHOUSE

Chuck Kruger

Chuck Kruger grew up in New York's
Finger Lakes. In protest against the Vietnam
War, he moved to Switzerland. Twenty-six
years later he moved to Cape Clear Island.
He is a regular on *Sunday Miscellany*, the *Quiet
Quarter*, *Seascapes* and NPR's *Weather Notebook*
(USA). http://indigo.ie/~ckstory/

Four miles to the west of Cape
Clear Island, and eight miles from
the mainland, rises the solitary Fastnet
Rock and its towering lighthouse. In
severe storms, even the 180-foot tip of
the Fastnet is sometimes obscured, not
only by the crests of mighty breakers,
but also by the waves themselves.
When foggy or misty, the Fastnet's
identifiable foghorn kicks in, a
comforting sound and focal point
from anywhere on Cape as visibility
approaches zero. At night the lantern's

bright flash of rotating light reassuringly sweeps the region at five-second intervals – a rhythm as recognisable to mariners as station identifications to radio listeners.

If there's one incontrovertible symbol of the southwest coast of Ireland, it's the Fastnet, its first tower lighting up in 1854, its present tower in 1904. John Feehan wrote: 'The wind that round the Fastnet sweeps blows in all its fury and in all its gentleness along the entire coast from Cork to the Mizen Head, and makes itself known in no uncertain terms to every yachtsman, every fisherman, every mariner who sails these seas, and there are few among them who have not the healthiest respect for it ... The gods that rule the seas are no playthings for us mortals.'

Last summer I had an entirely new experience of the Fastnet. I was fortunate to see it not only from up close but also, at last, from on the Rock itself.

Every summer this last decade or so I've made a point of taking an evening boat trip – or three – out to the Fastnet, repeatedly circling its looming eminence while clicking away with both camera and heart. On one trip last year we had dolphins leaping all around us, playing in the bow wave, frolicking in the wake and alongside. Whales we saw in the distance. And a pair of grey Atlantic seals out at the Fastnet itself.

Then, out of the blue last August, a couple of friends invited me along in their yacht, and when we got to the Rock, Barbara took the helm and Gerry, two other friends and I hopped aboard his dinghy, rowed right up to the Rock. Excited, I jumped for Charraig Aonair, made it without getting too wet, the swell exceptionally slight. I held the painter tight while the others took the leap. We prowled the Rock for an hour. I'd been meaning to do this for years, had many times read *The History of the Fastnet Rock Lighthouse*, by C. W. Scott, a 1904 book recently reissued in a facsimile edition by Schull Books of Ballydehob.

While the Lighthouse itself was locked up tight during our exploration, the tower having been automated back in 1989, we still had a chance to feel what it's like to be on the tiniest of islands well out to sea. I confess I was so smitten by the sensation of at last being on the Rock that I began to imagine what it would have been like to live there, to have been a lighthouse keeper, three weeks on, one week off, to have helped to build the edifice. A construction foreman once lived there for ten months straight.

For some, such a way of life might be like being in prison, an Irish Alcatraz, but for others, I now know, it can be a liberation, so close does one feel oneself — still earthed — to the inner workings of the sea.

THE KING OF KILKERRIN CASTLE

Mae Leonard

Mae Leonard, originally from The Parish, Limerick, now living in Co. Kildare, is a broadcaster and award-winning writer and poet. Her publications include *My Home Is There*, *This Is Tarzan Clancy* and *Six for Gold*.

Driving through Labasheeda in Co. Clare, I missed the turn-off for Killimer and a couple of miles later I found myself confronted by the Shannon with no way across or around it. The man who answered my knock on the cottage door told me that I was at Battery Point, Kilkerrin – a dead end – and directed me back to the main road. I turned to leave when he suddenly asked, 'Would you like to see my castle?'

I hesitated for a couple of seconds,

looked at his beaming face and sure what could I say only – Yes. Yes, please. He introduced himself as Barney and said that he was busy saving hay and had no time to show me around but gave me a large key and pointed to the stone roof just showing above a grassy hill. Following his instructions I walk the shoreline for a short distance, cross a style and go up through a sloping grassy field. The drawbridge is down and the key turns easily in the lock of the great wooden door. It creaks open. I enter into the gloom and feel my way around the wall until my eyes become accustomed to the darkness. I discover a stone stairway and climb up and out onto the battlements to command a magnificent view of Clonderlaw Bay and the broad Shannon Estuary all the way down to Carrigaholt. The ferry from Killimer chugs across, disturbing a school of dolphin leaping along the Tarbert Strait. And all the while the glorious scent of new-mown hay mingles with the turf smoke hanging on the Co. Clare air.

I suppose Barney's Castle could be called a Martello Tower because it was built as a defence against a possible invasion by Napoleon, but it's not a tower – it's a fort, a battery fort. The battery section is a semi-circular wall with star points where guns were once fitted and the whole arrangement is surrounded by a dry moat. And in the centre of the moat is a blockhouse about fifty feet long that has solid stone walls six or seven feet thick.

I wanted to see more but I was pressed for time and had reluctantly to leave Barney's Castle that day. However, he was at home on my return and he proudly explained to me how the fort was constructed from limestone that was ferried all the way down the river from Limerick. The main floors are of blue flagstone, quarried at Moneypoint further down the coast. The building is held together with a mortar mixture of ground granite, lime, ash, hot wax and ox blood. Up on the flat roof are a couple of depressed circles, each about two metres across, with an axle in the centre where high calibre howitzers once sat. The fort was completed, armed and had a garrison of twenty in 1814, by which time Napoleon had met his Waterloo and was no longer a threat. The guns were never fired at an enemy but at a training session one of the howitzers was loaded and the whole building shook with the force of the shot. The recoil damaged part of the main building. A crack formed in one wall and a steel cable had to be fitted around the entire building to support the wall, as well as to act as a lightning conductor. There are storerooms in the basement and a magazine cell for storing gunpowder and rifles.

Supplies were delivered by boat and winched up to the battery – part of an old iron winch still remains on the shore today. The soldiers planted vegetables in the fields surrounding the fort and they were known to join the locals for a pint in Labasheeda. In fact, *céilí* dances became a feature at the fort, and the garrison occasionally invited their counterparts from a similar fort across on the Tarbert side of the river. The invitations were delivered by semaphore. Both the battery forts were occupied until the end of the nineteenth century. The one at Tarbert was removed to make way for the ESB power station and so solidly was it built that it took eleven blasts of explosives to destroy it. In 1973 the government sold the Kilkerrin battery fort and its nine acres to its closest neighbour – Barney. Thus, he became the King of Kilkerrin Castle.

IRISH GIANTS
AT RISK

Thomas Pakenham

Thomas Pakenham is the author of highly
acclaimed works of history, including *The
Scramble for Africa* and *The Boer War*. He
achieved worldwide success several years
ago with the publication of *Meetings with
Remarkable Trees*, a collection of sixty individual trees in Britain and Ireland.

Henry Grattan, the eighteenth-century Irish statesman, has
always been a hero of mine. When his
agent told him that the safety of one
of his houses at his estate in County
Wicklow was threatened by a
magnificent beech tree, Grattan refused
to cut the tree down. 'I know that tree,'
he is supposed to have said. 'It means
no harm to anyone.'

Of course trees can be dangerous
and have to be removed. New suburbs
have to be built, new roads carved out

of the forest. But people are often indifferent to the price of this kind of progress. Or they do care, but it's too late. A great tree is taken for granted until the moment it is cut down, or blows down. Then we feel a pang of bereavement. But why had we never looked more closely at this giant on our doorstep? Perhaps that beech had been there for 200 years and knew the village many generations before it became a suburb. Or perhaps that oak was planted to mark some famous, or infamous, event. But nobody bothered to pass on the details of the oak's pedigree and now it's gone to the knackers'. Our failure to appreciate this part of our heritage makes a mockery of our supposed new respect for the environment. Why do we not use our eyes?

Consider the raw facts about trees. The giants of our native (and naturalised) species are the biggest living things on this island, heavier than any land animal, taller than most buildings, older than many ancient monuments. If a big tree were not a living organism, it would still be a remarkable object. A big oak or beech can weigh 30 tons, cover 2,000 square yards and include 10 miles of twigs and branches. Each year the tree pumps several tons of water 100 feet into the air, produces 100,000 leaves and covers half an acre of trunk, branches and roots with a new pelt of bark.

Yet the tree is alive and uniquely individual. There is no mass production; every tree, sexually conceived (as opposed to cloned), builds itself to a different design – as we see at first glance. No wonder that writers have so often admired, and stood in awe of, great trees. Turgenev, the Russian novelist, said that the sight of a pine forest filled him with a sense of his own nothingness. He said that after a walk in a forest he returned thankfully to his own world, where he 'dared believe in his own power and importance'. Herman Hesse, the German poet, found trees the most 'penetrating preachers'. As he put it: 'I revere them when they live in tribes and families, in forests and groves. And even more I revere them when they stand alone. They are like lonely persons.

Not like hermits who have stolen away out of some weakness but like great, solitary men, like Beethoven and Nietzsche.' Emerson said that in a wood, 'Man casts off his years as a snake his slough.' Restored to childhood in the silent temple of nature, he felt that, 'Nothing can befall me in life – no disgrace, no calamity, which nature cannot repair.'

Of course, a few writers have found the silence of trees not only awe-inspiring, but also frustrating. John Stewart Collis admitted as much. 'Their silence, their indifference to us, is almost exasperating. We would speak to them, we would ask their message – for they seem to hold some weighty truth, some special secret.' But for most people the opposite is true. We welcome the silence of trees. It is friendly and companionable. Trees make such excellent listeners. And, I assume, this was the great attraction to the numerous statesmen who have admired trees, from Henry Grattan onwards. After the hurly-burly of politics, it must be such a comfort to find an audience that doesn't answer back.

By the way, Grattan did decide to do something about the great beech tree that was overhanging his house in Wicklow. He told his agent to knock down the house that was threatening the tree.

THE CLADDAGH

Fred Johnston

Fred Johnston, born in Belfast in 1951, is the founder of Galway's Cúirt literature festival and of The Western Writers' Centre. A novelist, short-story writer, poet and critic, he was writer-in-residence at the Princess Grace Irish Library in Monaco in 2004.

In autumn, the light over Galway Bay is unique and mysterious. On a particularly magical day, the water glass-smooth, the air charged with an otherworldly silence, you wait with a growing feeling of expectation: something is about to happen at the edge of imagination's eye.

A door has opened, admitting this blue-gold light. It settles over the silver, rustling water. Over the Bay, the hills of Clare tremble in their dreaming sleep. A seabird, unsure of itself, flicks over the water and climbs upwards quickly, secure in higher air. The elements of air, earth, water, fire have combined to reveal a new world: everything around you has changed; a sudden and natural alchemy has altered the colour and texture of grass, water, rock. Too soon everything reverts to a quiet ordinariness – what we have come to consider as the real. But for that handful of moments, we had been given a glimpse of something eternal.

On one such evening, I walked under Spanish Arch, down Long Walk, the old harbour of the Claddagh on my right, the waters of the river rushing below me into the bay. Into the mouth of the harbour and the river came a small boat, a *púcán*, its sails tilting and full, gulping up every morsel of breeze out of the falling stillness. The motion of the boat, its full-sailed grace and dignity, made me stop and watch. Small voices drifted over the water. The boat curved and arced into the shelter of the harbour, coming home, natural in its every movement. The rust-red sails clapped in the breaths of wind, a sound of applause; the shiny black hull slid like a black beetle over the skin of the harbour. I was filled with an excited sense of vision, as if I were seeing something of great significance; as if such a moment would never come again. I was grateful to the boat, to the unknown men who crewed her; I envied them. Later I wrote a poem, 'Boat Dreaming', in which I gave the boat a human voice and let her explain herself.

I am what is on the sea
and below the sea and above the sea:
the sun is roped to my shoulder,
black my Pythagorean sail,
the wind is the breath
of the world in sleep –
I am hailed by name from the stone quay.

Now I lean over to let
the last hour of light wash the air;

GALWAY RAIN

Kate Duignan

Kate Duignan moved to Cork from
Bannockburn at thirteen and experienced
extreme culture shock (boarding school,
nuns, no boys), but since then considers
Ireland, specifically Galway, home. She
wants to move to the country once her two
children are on their way.

It was another dark winter evening. I
was waiting yet again for a bus that
was late. My feet were cold, I was tired
and then it began to rain. Beside me a
mother and daughter hailed a friend
pushing a buggy. They were from some
part of Africa and began to chat with
good humour. I was gradually
becoming damper and colder, cursing
the rain as had become my habit, when
I realised that the little girl was
entranced. She stood blinking the
raindrops off her thick lashes. She
opened her mouth and tilted back her

head to receive the drops. She held out her hands towards the wetness and, when she had enough collected, rubbed the rain all over her face.

She loved rain!

Stumbling along, a drunk approached the little group. 'Don't mind them ould cowboys up the town,' he bawled at them. 'You're alright, they're only cowboys.' He wandered off and then returned to hand a €2 piece to the little girl. One of the mothers asked if he had any money for her. He gave her a friendly thump on the arm. 'Go on out of that, do ya think I'm a millionaire? Don't mind them ould cowboys up the town,' he said again and made his way down the square. The women laughed and looked after him with wonder. The little girl clutched her treasure before being told to put her 'Irish money' safely in her pocket. The rain, the late bus, the insidious creeping dampness had all utterly vanished. I found that I had a smile on my face. I was still smiling as they left. Changed by the little girl's joy, her embracing of the water I take for granted falling from a Galway sky.

To quote a song from a woman called Honor Finnegan who lived here for a few years, 'You'd better love rain if you want to live in Galway.' It is a city of canals, branching from the rough strong flow of the River Corrib, which is fed by Lough Corrib. There is a huge area down the Claddagh called 'The Swamp'. This town is so wet, we have a street called 'Flood Street'. And it does flood at the spring tides. There are acres of bog out the road in Connemara where you can squeeze the moisture from the land like squeezing a sponge. All the trickles, torrents and drains make their way to the Atlantic which hugs the city in its salty arms. Even the rock sucks up the water before producing it again, like a magic trick, in the form of turloughs.

Some days the wind howls as if in torment as it travels and buffets the walls of the city. There are days when you can't hear because of the roar of big, fat, insistent raindrops on the roof and windscreen wipers make little difference to visibility. Plumes of water are driven towards pedestrians by cars troughing like speedboats through pools on the waterlogged road. Many times I have come home with sodden clothes after walking through a small typhoon between the bus stop and my door.

But the rain also cleanses and renews. It washes away the dog excrement and the vomit of last night. It keeps down the dust from the building sites. Sometimes the rain forces the builders to stop. Then the sound of jackhammers and the whine of cranes, the clash of metal against stone and the engines of the dumper trucks, stop. Peace slips in, filling the alleys and lanes with echoes of precipitation.

My attitude to the wateriness of Galway has definitely changed since that encounter on Eyre Square, when I observed the relish with which the little girl rubbed the rain onto her sunny skin. The day when buckets of good old Galway rain greeted her with gusto. Now at the wet bus stop, I find myself humming the lines of a song by Pádraig Stevens: 'The rain comes lashing, splish splashin' down the town in a Galway fashion.'

THE CALL OF
THE MOUNTAINS

Margaret Lee

Margaret Lee was born in Ballingarry, Co.
Limerick, the youngest of eight children.
She works as a social worker and presently
lives in Newport, Co. Tipperary, with
Fidel and Baba Dubh.

Vive La France! No, I don't work for
the French Tourist Board, but
when it comes to holidays, my thoughts
usually turn to France: cycling around
the rugged northern coast of Brittany;
lolling on a beach in the Vendee region;
hill-walking in the Pyrenees; sight-
seeing in Paris. Now, in the long hot
summer of 2003, our chosen destination is the French Alps and on the first
hike we are heading for the Pointe de la
Sambuy. When I look ahead I am
gazing into the mountains; when I
pause for breath and look back the Lac
d'Annecy is spread out beneath me.

Mountains have always held a fascination for me. I was reared in the shadow of Knockfierna, which was the highest knoll that the flat farmland of west Limerick could claim as its own. As a child I was told that it was the home of the fairies, that they came out at night, danced, frolicked, made merry and vanished into thin air when the sun rose. As an adult I climbed to its summit and looked down on the Shannon Estuary. The climb was easy, effortless, little more than a stroll, very different from this steep ascent to the Pointe de la Sambuy.

It is the thoughts that are remarkably similar. I am thinking of how the word 'hill' has become a metaphor in our day-to-day lives. We talk about some of our endeavours as being 'uphill all the way', denoting struggle, persistent effort to achieve something that does not come easily. Then when the goal is achieved, it's 'down hill', it's easy. Or maybe the goal is never achieved because we have set our sights on the impossible, or others say that it is impossible, but we know better, we know that it is out there somewhere. Well, alright, it can't be achieved here and now, but if we lived somewhere else, had a different job, held a different qualification, we would attain that elusive goal. 'Far away hills' are always greener.

Maybe we would realise our elusive dream if other people did not get in our way. That person who won't retire, who is blocking a talented person like me from promotion – well, he is 'over the hill'. And maybe I too am over the hill. But I am learning that 'over the hill' has compensating aspects, that there is more shelter, a clearer view, an unexpected vista. 'Over the hill' means that you have been there, that you have reached the summit. Like Martin Luther King, you have 'been to the mountain', you have seen 'the Promised Land'.

We push on. Pointe de la Sambuy is within reach, but the climb is arduous and risky. We keep going. The summit is worth the strenuous hike. I think about other, easier climbs. But it's all a matter of scale. Knockfierna was small but loomed large in my West Limerick childhood because there was no other hill to compete with it. It was easy to reach the top, like some of my early goals now seem to me. They too now seem small, unimportant even, but at the time they appeared large and significant: passing that exam, getting that job, being accepted by that in-group. My happiness depended on their achievement. And some I did achieve, others not. Now none of them seems to matter very much. Their import has vanished, gone, as ephemeral as the fairies in a Knockfierna dawn. I can see that their pursuit sometimes kept me from seizing the opportunities that lay around me. But the mountains remain and speak to us of the landscape of our childhood. Once, when travelling overnight from London to Limerick, the voice of an elderly woman echoed through the bus on the outskirts of Clonmel. 'Soon we will see Sliabh na mBan.' While there was expectancy, nostalgia and a certain melancholy in her tone, she was telling us that she was entering her own place.

And myself? I will persist, arduous though the climb is. I will get to the Pointe de la Sambuy. Because Knockfierna has become a part of me, the hills will always call me on. The lure of the summit gives me life.

MOSNEY

Donal O'Kelly

Donal O'Kelly is a playwright and actor and has performed his solo plays such as *Catalpa*, *Bat the Father Rabbit the Son* and *Jimmy Joyced!* to high acclaim throughout the English-speaking world. He founded the human rights theatre company Calypso Productions and is an associate director of the peace and human rights organisation Afri.

When I was about eight or nine, I was brought to Butlins holiday camp in Mosney for a day-trip. Around the corner of the last chalet the vast panorama of amusement machines revealed itself. I can still remember the surging thrill of it. Then an even greater shock: you could go on everything for free. It was like paradise. My sisters and cousins flapped into the middle of it like moths to a lamp. I wandered towards the tumbling, spinning machines. The choice was so enormous I was paralysed. Paralysed by freedom. I just couldn't make my mind up.

There were carousels and swingboats, big, high, well-oiled swings, bumper-cars, this kind of swingy-thing, that kind of bumpy-thing. They were like big, garish monsters having a party, legs and arms going up and down and in and out. The whole thing was so fantastic it was overwhelming.

I had to sit down. There was a little wooden kerb. I sat down to try to gather my wits and figure out what I should do. I raised my eyes to look up at the sky. And that was when I saw it. It was the most beautiful thing.

A window up high in a concrete wall. And people were swimming in it. They were underwater whooping around and treading water, diving into view and swimming out again. It was mesmerising. I couldn't drag myself away. I watched for hours. My mother and my aunt tried to encourage me to try a few things. But all I wanted was to look at the people swimming in the window. I figured out who was friends with whom; who was whose daddy; and that two of them were a boyfriend and girlfriend because he kept smiling at her underneath the water. I think he was trying to talk because bubbles came out of his mouth. And they all bobbed around up there, under the water, doing some of kind of crazy slow-motion acrobatics and holding their breaths.

Recently, I had reason to go back to that holiday camp in Mosney for the first time since that day in the mid-1960s. It was to see the ballroom, with a view to putting on a performance of Roddy Doyle's play *Guess Who's Coming for the Dinner* by Calypso. Roddy's play is about a girl bringing a Nigerian asylum-seeker to her Dublin home to meet her father. It's funny. It's also timely and provocative.

What was Butlins Mosney is now the Asylum-Seekers' Dispersal Centre Mosney. Five hundred people live there. No free monster-machine parties now. And I couldn't find the underwater window. But there were people of over forty nationalities. Every colour of the human rainbow. Some looking well-installed, making the best of it presumably. Some walking slowly like ghosts.

The disused ballroom echoes with the voices and big-band sounds of the sixties and seventies. The beautiful parquet oak floor is pockmarked with the swivels of countless stilettos. In the dim work-lights it laps in silence like a calm dark sea.

Outside, the involuntary residents from across the seas exist as best they can. They have full board, which means breakfast, dinner and tea, and television in every chalet. They also receive fifteen pounds per week for incidental expenses. And a bus goes to Drogheda daily, where the nearest library is. The atmosphere is a bit different from the throbbing excitement of thirty-odd years ago.

One of the residents I spoke to has been there ten months, with still no date set for an interview to assess his claim for political asylum. Apart from wanting a cap placed on the length of time one has to wait, his biggest worry is to be sent to another dispersal centre. The people who have been in Mosney for any length of time know that it's the best they can expect under the terms of the Department of Justice's direct provision and dispersal policy. They are afraid that they could be sent to a caravan in Kildare Barracks or in the middle of nowhere outside Athlone. Or worse. Word travels fast among people in trouble. Especially bad word. And there are dispersal centres in Ireland, faraway from Mosney, faraway from home, where vulnerable people dread to be sent.

TREES

Kevin Connolly

Kevin Connolly grew up in England and
Bailieborough, Co. Cavan, and is the
owner-founder of The Winding Stair
Bookshop in Dublin.

What is it about trees that
entrances us? That delights us?
That grieves us when they are damaged
or callously removed? That pacifies us?
That stirs within us a docile acceptance of their existence?

Is it their sentient, innocent wisdom? Is it their stubborn tranquillity,
sustained in spite of our efforts to
create a maelstrom of activity about
them? Is it even their inhumanity or the
peace that creaks from them in which
the universe can be contemplated in
awe and astonishment?

Once, trees covered 60 per cent of
the world's land surface. Now it is
closer to 6 per cent. Mankind has been

almost exclusively responsible for this denudation of the planet. We have razed, and continue to raze, huge tracts of forest. However, we would not be the society we are today without having done so. Most of our European forests were already decimated by the end of the seventeenth century and it is a symptom of civilisation everywhere that we alter our landscapes in the pursuit of progress. Witness the wholesale demolition of avenues of trees across the country in the interests of road-alignment.

However, this does not need to be one-way traffic. Richard Jefferies, the English naturalist, believed that each one of us should be responsible for the planting of at least one deciduous tree in each of our lifetimes. There is a sense of selfless yet overwhelmingly satisfying retribution in the planting of new trees. It is a timeless, unconditional gesture – a gift to the future and to those who will occupy it. To this end, wherever I go, I collect seeds, cuttings, saplings and plant them wherever I find the space to do so. A small field in County Sligo is now a small wood with chestnut (horse, red and Spanish), alder, ash, oak, beech, birch and the ubiquitous, but no less worthy for that, sycamore.

For the last fifteen years or so, I have grown trees there. Those years have witnessed the gradual evolution of a new and exciting world within the field; the emergence of a rich and varied eco-system. Birds, other animals, insects and plants thrive and shelter under the trees' leafy foliage. In this field a quiet world has emerged beneath the lengthening boughs where the luminous vortices of colour converge and dance with the daylight to create hushed secret places. Amongst these shadows glides a universe, the north and south of it; the east and west of it; the latitude and longitude and length and breadth of it; the infinite boundless beauty of it; the four winds and the sacred space of it; the knowing and unknowing and the succulent promise of it; the silence and the deep, primeval hum and unfathomable mystery of it.

Here too is the space to allow my often-occluded sense of wonder the opportunity to simply 'be' and to marvel. Amongst

MIDLANDS

Edward Denniston

Edward Denniston, a native of Longford, teaches in Newtown School in Waterford where he has lived since 1980. He has published one book of poems, entitled *The Point Of Singing*.

A place you go through, not to' was the response of a gently spoken English lady on hearing that I was originally from the midlands. She, inevitably, was driving west across – or through – the centre of the country to be near mountain and seascape. It's very difficult to recommend a place or landscape you have affection for without sounding like a voice-over for a short promotional video, particularly if the landscape is regarded as featureless. I like what the Australian farmer/poet Les Murray says: 'Near void of feature always moves me, but not to thought; it lets me rest from thinking.'

On Sunday drives with my father, what I remember is how beautiful and exotic it seemed when we came across a narrow road that gently descended onto a short floodplain and then narrowed even further before buckling up across a small, solid limestone bridge, beneath which a slow flowing river meandered.

I remember thinking that we might drive forever, caught in the centrifugal force of fields, ditches and laneways, never to end up in coastal or mountainous counties, like Wicklow or Kerry — names that conjured up the truly exotic.

The poet C. Day Lewis used the phrase 'memories fructified in the dark'. The essence of this was made strikingly real for me recently when, as a result of being asked to do a reading on the borders of Co. Westmeath and Longford, a whole crowd of images and associations began to inveigle their way into my workaday thinking. And all these had to do with what must have been to me an exotic place on the shore of the Shannon. While moving through these images in my head it occurred to me, quite suddenly, that a number of years ago I'd been thinking about the same place and that somewhere I'd scribbled down notes in an attempt to hold onto the pictures that were, at that time, re-emerging. I searched through a pile of yellowing papers and found my scribblings. Many of the images in what I like to think will be one of a number of midland poems are from these long forgotten notes. When I read a draft of the poem outdoors on a sunny Sunday afternoon at Goldsmith's birthplace, a lady whispered to me afterwards, without any sense of drama or emphasis, 'I recognise the big car and the flowery deck-chairs.' It turns out they belonged to her parents.

Elfeet Bay : Lough Ree

Spread a green tartan rug on a patch of closely cropped grass
surrounded by clumps of rush between the frothy shore
and a ditch of whitethorn blazed with whin.

From the boot of the black *Anglia* take out a cake tin,
blue crockery, flask, *Tupperware* sandwich box —
from the rear windscreen, a coloured ball, sticky and hot.

Across the lake on the Roscommon shore watch out
for the sun-flash on car glass — a signal from other lives;
listen for words from a rowboat heading for an island,

drifting shoreward, and the splash of oars on water,
and on a transistor, the runaway voice of *Micheál O'Hehir*
urging a ball through the air as you dander down-shore

to an inlet, where piles of sun-toasted kipeens
are washed up from a reed bed that sways
and catches the light at the mouth of the lake.

Turn away from screaming swimmers who smash
the water's glassy surface; pass the big *Ford Zephyr*
under the sycamore, where a wicker basket

sits between two flowery deck-chairs; stroll the lane
to the outhouse that's dark and cool and smelling of hay;
return slowly through a field of cows;

emerge at a hole in the ditch just at the spot
where they've gathered, ready for tea, as swimmers
shiver, hug themselves from the chill of the lake.

Sit quietly on the tartan rug; wonder about mums and dads
and boys and girls who gather at a sandy spot, in a field
by a lake, on a hot summer's day; wonder

how long the *Shannon* is —
all the way down to the sea that can't be imagined,
like the highest mountain in Ireland.

LIVING IN THE
IRISH SEA

Carl Tighe

Carl Tighe was born in Birmingham in 1950. He has published the fiction collections *Rejoice and Other Stories* and *Pax: Variations* and the novels *Burning Worm* and *KsssS: A Tale of Sex, Money and Alien Invasion.* His non-fiction includes *The Politics of Literature* and *Gdansk.* He currently teaches Creative Writing at the University of Derby.

When you live at the edge of a community, alliances and identities are always uncertain. You can feel the world shifting under you, like an irregular sea swell.

My Granma lived in the fishermen's cottages on the sea wall at Ringsend. It was with her we stayed. The cottage was very crowded and once Granma, to get us out from under her feet while she prepared dinner, asked my brother and I to step into the garden and pluck up a bunch of her home-grown carrots. We sprang to it and returned a few minutes later, having carefully shaken off the dirt, with about a dozen carrots, and we presented them to Granma. Looking back, I realise she wanted us out of the cottage because she was having some kind of a confab with my Dad. She took one look at the carrots and began to slap us about the head and face. She chased us from the kitchen. My father jumped into her path shouting: 'Ma, what are you doing? You asked them to pick the carrots.'

Granma was having none of it. She snatched up the carrots and shook them at my father. 'See,' she yelled. 'See! That's exactly what I'm talking about.'

My father was silent.

'You've brought a little tribe of Brummies into the world. Little Brummie savages. What were you thinking of, over there? Did you take leave of your senses?'

My brother and I retreated to the sea wall. My brother was wheezing with asthma. This was hard for us. I was nine, he was seven. We always found it difficult to understand why our Dublin family called us their English cousins. It put us at a distance. Englishness was not something we felt comfortable with, though, yes, we had Birmingham accents. But we were brought up in an Irish Catholic environment. We were surrounded by other Irish Catholic families. We went to an Irish Catholic school with nuns and priests and Irish Catholic teachers. We went to mass where our priest, Father Murphy, was a fierce Texan Irishman. And we did the penance he dished out. In what way were we less the real thing than him? If anything, our upbringing had been intensely Irish, but in a complicated immigrant way.

But what made it hard was that I was still limping from incidents the previous week. I was limping because I had been attacked in the playground by a gang – the James Boys, they called themselves – who said my brother and I were English. In fact the James Boys, like me, were Irish kids with Birmingham accents.

That same afternoon as I was going home, because I could not run I was cornered by another gang. They punched and kicked me until I slid down the wall and then kicked me in the chest, screaming: 'Irish Scum Bastard! Irish Scum Bastard!' My brother, unable to help, watched from a distance. When they had gone, he helped me home. After a week the bruises were ripe and yellow.

After two beatings in one day – one for being English, the other for being Irish – Granma's revelation that there was some ambiguity about us did not come entirely as a surprise. That it came from Granma, that she blamed my father, that somehow my mother was nowhere in this picture – these were real, lasting, painful messages. My brother and I were here: we were facts. That we were not what was required, well, there was nothing I could do about that.

PEOPLE

DEATH AND MEMORY

Máiride Woods

Máiride Woods, originally from Co.
Antrim, lives in Dublin and has published
and won awards for her short stories,
features and poems, including two
Hennessy Awards, the Francis McManus
Award and the National Women's Poetry
Competition. She has been involved with
disability for many years.

Some people think of Lourdes when
they hear the word 'miracle'; some
people think of the marriage feast of
Cana; but I think of an afternoon in a
blue-toned coffee shop called
Jonathan's, almost thirty years ago. It
was some months after we got the bad
news about Aoife – our only child at
the time. In those days doctors were
slow to diagnose disability, but when
Aoife was almost three, we had to
accept that her not walking, not

talking, her constant hand-clapping meant handicap, as it was called in those days. Get her onto a waiting list, we were told, as she smiled up at us, oblivious to her fate. It was obvious that she needed me, her mother; what was less obvious was how much I depended on her.

Why do I write about Aoife? To remember her, to tell others about her, to scratch her name on the sky. Aoife never won medals, never painted pictures or sang songs. But she liked people; she liked stories and songs. She loved oranges and Leonard Cohen. Our daughter died in April 2001. Quite suddenly in her sleep, the way most of us would wish to go, but to the immense grief of all the family. After her death one of the nicest things was the number of people who told me about their special relationship with her and her beautiful smile. People like Aoife lead lives more hidden than Thérèse's ever was in the Carmel of Lisieux. But hidden lives sometimes have more meaning than outwardly successful ones.

It's not always easy being a mother to a disabled child. I sometimes felt frustrated at how little she could do and how restricted I was. There was such a lot to cram into the time she was at her day-centre, into the days of respite time. Part of me felt guilty at my failure in devotion, while another part felt obscurely that both of us needed me to go out and discover new and interesting things. In the weeks after her death that Sinead O'Connor song kept repeating itself in my head: 'Since you've been gone, I can do whatever I want ... But nothing compares to you.' I had no desire any more to eat my dinner in a fancy restaurant or do the other things I had sometimes hankered after in the past.

Dependency, I think, is a two-way thing – I depended on Aoife almost as much as she did on me. Because she had been born when I was in my early twenties, she was the link to the magic time of my own youth. And as my other children grew up and became aware of my imperfections, the love that I saw when

she fixed her eyes on mine was infinitely more precious. Losing
her has been a dismantling of myself.

The idea of forgetting her seems horrendous.

The Weirdness of Dead Infantas

There is shrouded space beside me
That people leave free; not wanting to intrude
Or get too close; grief's easier in Emily Dickinson,
Short lines and distance. This space
Is wheelchair shaped and I keep checking it
In case your ghost is hungry.
Another mouthful? No resistance,
When spoon meets empty air. As always you're
Silent as the grave, though now and then I catch
The random shimmer of your sounds.
The words I used to speak for you
Lie crumbling at the bottom of my bag,
Not thrown out, still powdering everything. How's
The best girl in the world?
Not in the world, I think, remembering
That Portuguese prince who travelled with his dead Infanta,
Propping her beside him
On foreign thrones. How weird,
That guidebook said, but I am not so sure …
Forgetfulness is weirder.

STONES

Mary O'Donnell

Mary O'Donnell's novels include *The Light-Makers*, *Virgin and the Boy* and *The Elysium Testament*. She has published four poetry collections, including *Spiderwoman's Third Avenue Rhapsody*, *Unlegendary Heroes* and, more recently, *September Elegies*. She is a member of Aosdána.

Sometimes, my daughter and I lie in bed pretending to be stones. Yes, stones. The game has developed from a starting point where I was trying to get her to keep her feet still in the bed to something more involved. The idea is that we lie folded into one another and say nothing for a while. After a time, one of us might pass a comment, from the point of view of a smooth stone on a beach, for example. The beach stones are our favourite kind. Sometimes, she remarks on a seagull that has just passed overhead, or the sound of a ship far out from the shore. All kinds of things happen on that imaginary beach among the stones. Sometimes we are walked over by crabs, their claws clacking as they scurry sideways across our greyness; tiny insects move around us, beneath us, sometimes armies of ants file across us, on their way to some definite ant-ish goal.

What we like best is the incoming tide.

'Is it near? Is it getting near?' my daughter whispers in my ear, her whole body quite still.

'Not yet. Not yet. Yes, it's coming, I can hear it, the water is coming!' I whisper back.

Then we wait again.

'It's gone back,' I say forlornly. 'It was too soon.'

'There's a black-back gull up there,' she remarks with a sigh, as we wait for the tide. 'Ugh!' she shudders, almost forgetting that she is a stone. 'It just dropped something horrible on me! Yeuch!'

'Uh-uh ...' I mutter. 'Look what's coming!'

'Oh no!' she hisses, alarmed.

We are always alarmed when people approach, because people, it is understood, can pick us up and throw us away from one another. Into the deep, up closer to the base of the cliff where we will never feel the tide running across our greyness.

'It's OK, they've gone,' she says with relief.

Finally, the tide washes in. It's as if we have waited all our lives for the salty water, the clear, bubbling, embracing silk of that first wave, and as it finally gushes over us, drenching us, we sigh with delight, restored by the scents and wetness of the ocean, from which we know everything has come.

After the tide has flooded over us, it inevitably retreats, but there is pleasure in that too. After the wetness, we look forward to dryness, to the wind shaping our curves, smoothing our roughness, keeping us primed in our stoniness, and to the sun, which we know will make us expand gently. Sometimes we make creaking sounds, as the sun warms our deep stone layers.

Recently, I realised that when we play Stones, we are

unconsciously mimicking some of the things that have always affected people: the necessity to respond to change, for example, the dread of ugliness, of violence, the need for replenishment by a force outside the smallness of our own concerns; the pleasure taken in intuitively reading what is going on around us. And being stones and fairly permanent, we try to live forever in one moment, just enjoying it for what it is.

I NEVER SANG
FOR MY FATHER

Ken Bruen

Ken Bruen was born and now lives in
Galway, has a Ph.D. in metaphysics and
was jailed in Brazil. In recent years his
crime novels featuring alcoholic ex-guard
Jack Taylor have met with critical and
commercial success.

I've read so many accounts of the
father/son relationship. Among the
best are Blake Morrison and Tony
Parsons. Years ago, I saw a movie on
television starring Melvyn Douglas
and Gene Hackman.

You want to talk harrowing!
Phew-oh.

Gene Hackman, as the son, can
never please his father. Boy does he try.

After, I sat with my head in my
hands, said, Oh God.

In my novels, fathers get a rough
deal. They're usually

Violent

Cruel

Alcoholic

My Dad was none of these.

In all my lost years, he never once turned away. I believed I could never impress him. He understood success in monetary terms. When my second book was displayed in Foyle's window, I must have walked Charing Cross Road a hundred times.

Rang my father. He asked, 'How much did they pay you?'

'It doesn't work like that.'

'Why?'

On receiving my Ph.D., I called him. He said, 'If you think you'll be called *Doctor* in this house, you can kiss my arse.'

After he died, beside his bed, I found copies of all my books. Interspersed through the well-thumbed pages, was every review I'd ever had.

One of my earliest memories is him sweeping all the furniture in the kitchen to the side. Then taking my mother's hand he danced her the length and breath of the room. I can still hear her laughing as she said, 'Ya big eejit.'

He said to me, 'Women will forgive a good dancer most anything.'

—I'm still testing the validity of that.

It was a Monday morning my mother rang me. She said, 'Your father has fallen — he hit his forehead.'

I got up there straight away. He was in bed, sitting up. It tore my heart to see the cut above his eye. He asked, 'How's the writing?'

'There's talk of them filming one of the books.'

'Don't let them cod you.'

The doctor came, arranged for an ambulance. The way things are, the wait was lengthy. My mother brought him tea and he said, 'I hope you didn't put sugar in.'

'Do I ever?'

— For the best part of forty years, he always said that.

I asked, 'Why?'

He gave a huge smile, said, 'Ary, it keeps her on her toes.'
Later, he asked me to get his wallet from his pants. I did. He used
banks but didn't rely on them. Out came hundreds of pounds. He
said, 'Mind that for me.'

'I will.'

The effortless trust was perhaps his best review. I went in the
ambulance with him and he said, 'I'm fierce trouble to you.'

That was Monday. On Thursday he was in good spirits, said,
'They do lovely jelly with the dinner.'

'I hate jelly.'

'Ah, you only think that.'

He'd contradict the devil. The last thing he said, 'They're letting
me home tomorrow.'

He died on Friday morning. With my mother, I counted out
the bank notes. There was £630.

The reception after the funeral was at a Salthill hotel. I knew
he'd like us to hear the waves roar. The manager asked if we'd any
specifications for the meal. I said, 'No jelly.'

The bill came to … £628. I'll never forget the fierce pride in
my mother's eyes as she said, 'Your Dad – he was a great man to
price a job.'

FORTY-FOUR

Michael Murtagh

Michael Murtagh was born in 1958 and
brought up in Crossmaglen, Co. Armagh.
He has been a priest of Armagh Arch-
diocese since 1986. Vice-President of
County Louth Archaeological and Histor-
ical Society, he lectures in local history and
has a weekly column in the regional
newspaper *The Argus*.

Today I celebrate my forty-fourth
birthday. I begin my forty-fifth
year. My birthday happens to fall on
Lady Day, or Annunciation Day. I was
christened Gabriel on this account. I
became known by my second name,
Michael. Gabriel was considered a
little pretentious. It was also subject to
all sorts of unpleasant abbreviations. It
could have been worse. I might have
been called Annunciato.

The New Year began on this date
in England until the middle of the

eighteenth century. It was called Lady Day. All leases and contracts were dated from that day. In the wider world it had been considered the beginning of the year until the Gregorian calendar reforms in 1582 changed the date to 1 January. In the year 1958, Lady Day, for me, was the beginning of my contract with the world, my lease of life.

The very mention of the year 1958 makes me feel like a relic of the middle of the last century. Sometimes I try to remember how the forty-somethings of my childhood appeared to my infant eyes. They seemed to be parent-like and very old, I suppose. Though my elders tell me that I'm still 'only a child', I realise that from the perspective of a child I am something of an antiquity, being able to remember the beginnings of cultural disorder in the 1960s. I slept through the last years of the 1950s, thankfully, so I escaped the great whinge as a writer's theme. The sixties arrived in the 1970s where I lived.

In spite of the protestations of those of more mature years, I recognise the signs of wear and tear. In fact, my dentist told me some time ago that my teeth were uncommonly worn for someone of my years. I wondered on the reason and found comfort in telling myself that it could be worse. If I had been a horse, my valuation would be significantly decreased by worn teeth. There is a crease too that used not to be there and that appears at a right angle to my jaw-line in times of tiredness or weakness. It goes away, but some of these days I expect it to carve itself permanently into my features. My hair has gone grey, or just gone, and no amount of bottled promise can regain the dark brown or the blonde of my earlier and earliest years. I genuflect in an empty church and my knee cracks loudly. I hunch at a hospital bedside and cannot arise without pain and stiffness in my knees. I can no longer sleep the marathon of my student days, lazing and turning till dinnertime. Daybreak finds me awake and late nights leave me shattered.

There is a process of development to be gone through by those who reach these years. It is sometimes called trans-valuation by psychologists. It simply means that the outlook and values of youth are left behind or sought to be left behind. The youthful focus on the future, the fearlessness and the idealism of early adult life, usually give way to compromise, conservatism, conformity and pragmatism. Reputation may increase but ability declines. People who have difficulty negotiating this change or accepting the inevitable call the syndrome a 'mid-life crisis'. Those who deny the reality or fail to negotiate it safely often end up the butt of ridicule or may find themselves lying on the psychiatrist's couch, unable to accept their limitations and their mortality. There is the recognised figure of the 'oldest swinger in town', the bald male with the ponytail and earrings, wearing a jean-jacket and bovver boots and boasting of his latest conquest or purchase, occasionally meaning the same object. As the country song has it, 'the only difference between men and boys is the size of their shoes and the price of their toys'.

To whom does the term 'middle-aged' belong? I have no desire to claim it, as it reeks of cardigans and Brylcreem and Deep Heat. The psalmist tells us that the span of man is 'seventy years, or eighty for those who are strong'. He adds pessimistically, or with realism, that 'most of these are emptiness and pain. They pass swiftly and we are gone.'

Without claiming the labels of middle age, I have to admit, as Bill Clinton said some years ago, that I have, in all probability, more yesterdays than tomorrows. 'Only a fool celebrates getting older,' said another American so, on Lady Day, I will celebrate life and say with one of my favourite writers, Dag Hammerskjold, 'for all that has been – thanks – to all that will be – yes'.

I MY FATHER ON ACHILL ISLAND

John F. Deane

John F. Deane, born on Achill Island, now
writes poetry full time. He is a founder of
Poetry Ireland and a member of Aosdána.
His latest collection *Manhandling the Deity*
was published in 2003.

It was late summer, we were on
holiday on Achill Island and the
weather was, to be kind to it,
demanding. We had brought my father,
then some seventy-nine years old, and
on that day we decided we would eat
lunch and then go to Keem Bay and see
what was what. So, we had a delightful
meal of fresh salmon and brown bread
while the slow mists continued to
move by, like a procession of silent
ghosts, outside. By the time we got
back from the beautiful Keem Bay, the
mist had eased but the world remained
grey and damp. We waited a while and

then, perhaps out of sheer bravado, my daughter and I decided we'd brave the Atlantic Ocean and swim. We pronounced the water tolerable and then, to my wonder and delight, father decided he'd try it too. He undressed, braved the waves, got down and got out very quickly indeed and I could see him dress rapidly, then lean back against a rock to smoke. He was shivering with the cold and I felt very guilty indeed. That was, in fact, the last time he ever went in for a swim.

But it all came back to me as I watched him gaze vacantly out to sea, towards the mountains of the west, towards Croagh Patrick. I remembered those games he had initiated for us when we were children, games on that very beach, thought up to help us get dry and warm again after our swim. He would draw a great circle on the sand with a stick, then criss-cross the circle with easy paths. Right in the middle of the circle he placed a stone. The game consisted of running as fast as we could, keeping always to the lines he had drawn, trying to get to that stone before he tipped us with a seaweed stick. We loved the game and, of course, it dried us quickly and warmed us up. So that day I found myself doing exactly the same to help get myself and my daughter dry and warm, although this time my father would take no part. But that smile on his face, that proud stance, told me he was pleased and I saw myself at once as growing into my father, the way we all do, over the years, grow into our parents, assuming their idiosyncrasies, their ideas, their lives almost.

And does not this awareness remind us how circular is our living, even though we think we are moving forward in a straight line, as an individual, as a nation, as a race? How circular everything is, how the ending of our lives seems to join up full circle with our beginnings and how we are taught that, while time can be represented as a straight line, eternity is a circle.

You came into the game from a starting point near the rocks and ran, trying to reach the stone placed at the centre, the den, the safehouse, home; and there I go – screaming round the outermost circle, father pounding after, a switch of sea-wrack in his hand. Eternity, he told me once, is like the letter O; it has no beginning and no end, or like the nought, perhaps, and you could slither down and down through its black centre. With a silver pin he would draw the periwinkles from their shells, that soft flesh uncoiling from the whorl; he would scoop out that gravely meat from the barnacle and we swallowed its roundness whole with that black mucous-like blob at its centre. And see me now, following, the way you became your father, that same diffidence and turning inwards, that same curving of the spine, the way the left shoulder lifts in emphasis. See me where I run, my father watching from the distance as I go pounding round the outermost circle, a father myself, my child racing and laughing in front of me, and a switch of sea-wrack in my hand.

FOOTBALL WITH THE ANCESTORS

George Szirtes

George Szirtes was born in Budapest in
1948 and arrived in England as a refugee
after the revolution of 1956. He has
written many books of poems and edited
or translated various others.

I like football, the European kicking
and heading variety, but that may be
because I was introduced to it early by
my father. We went to the national
stadium together and watched a double
bill. In one of the matches a team in
red and blue played a team in deep
lilac. I didn't know adults could be so
colourful and so excited together.
About five years later I played the game
myself, in another country, on a muddy
school pitch. The mud clogged my
boots and running was hard but I
enjoyed it. I had found the first thing I
wanted to be very good at. I practised

in the garden, in the street and in the playground after school hours. I practised with others and by myself. I went to matches in London at various grounds, sometimes with my father, sometimes with friends, occasionally alone. And in the meantime I followed the teams on television, chose my own allegiance and gave my fearful devotion to the objects of it. It was as if all my hopes and energies could be focused and driven by one potent emblem: the team, its name, its colours, its personalities, their fortunes and misfortunes. Sometimes I fantasised about playing with them, or playing for my country (and which country would that be?), but secretly I had come to terms with reality. If I couldn't always be guaranteed a place in the school first team I was probably not that good. Doing became absorbed in the larger act of watching.

The teams embodied rivalries that, in my foreignness, I only slowly became aware of. These rivalries were partly local and partly based on envy. Arsenal and Tottenham were natural contenders for the nearby local patch. My team was elsewhere, in the distant north of the country, but was hated and envied elsewhere. It was harsh. Occasionally, the sheer viciousness of the rivalry surprised me. There were powerful displaced energies at play: the more powerful the energy the stronger, the more intoxicating the feeling. On one of my early returns to Hungary I met a poet whose drive I felt came partly from hatred of those who had mistreated or frustrated her in the past. The power of the feeling was channelled into the making of remarkable, disciplined poems that opened on deep, almost geological, inner landscapes.

There was a role, it seemed, for resentment. It could flow quickly from one pole to another. From negative to positive. In the same way the mood of a football crowd changes from despair and hatred to a vast, deeply moving joy which is somehow uplifting and consoling. We are tribal beings. We sing our histories and seek in them the most intoxicating and productive of energies.

Too abstract, all this. I wanted chiefly to talk about the

THE SEWING
MACHINE

Mary J. Byrne

Mary J. Byrne was born in Co. Louth, has
worked in Ireland, England, Germany and
Morocco and now lives in France. She has
had short stories broadcast and published
in Ireland and internationally. She is a
Hennessy Literary Award winner and
recipient of the Bourse Lawrence Durrell
de la Ville d'Antibes.

There was a Yugoslav couple on the
train back to Paris from Vienna.
He was anxious to exercise his French.
His wife just sat and smiled. They'd
been back home in Yugoslavia for
years, retired now on a small French
pension, but still kept a little room in
Paris that he'd bought years ago, a tiny
space in which he and his wife had
brought up their daughter. Like all
Yugoslavs, they had sent money down
home and little by little machinery was

bought for the farm and the house was improved. In Paris, he and his wife worked in sweatshops, kept an industrial sewing machine in the small room to make extra money, washed at the sink and used the toilet on the stairs. When they retired, they went home to help on the farm. 'My wife's a good woman,' he said, 'she cooks and sews.' His wife smiled and nodded, with little French despite the Paris years. The farm was ten hectares, about twenty-five acres. His brother bred white cows with yellow patches that produced up to twenty-five litres of milk a day. I wondered what lay in store for such a farm, in the new global economy.

It appeared that Yugoslavs never leave their country behind. His daughter left France as soon as her schooling was finished and married a young man down home. Sometimes these marriages were arranged in Paris. One girl had refused to return to the village. 'Too proud,' he said. That marriage had broken up. Yugoslav family solidarity seemed remarkable, as was the willingness of the children and grandchildren to follow their parents' ways. When a livelihood had to be found for his newly married daughter and her husband, the whole family sat down together and asked themselves, 'What is it that people always need – war or no war, prosperity or not?' The answer, they decided, was bread. So they opened up a little bakery on the farm, regular orders, people came to collect. 'It isn't easy,' he said. 'You have to work nights, seven days a week.' The grandson will take it over when finished his military service, so that their daughter and her husband can take a rest after twenty years. I thought it didn't sound like a family to rest much.

'That Slobo,' he said. He waved his arm in the air then stopped. 'But Yugoslavia will pick up again. We're Europeans. Tito knew how to hold us together. It was communism that ruined all those other countries,' he said. 'They all became robbers, even their new politicians.'

When the tirade was over, we enquired, by way of conversation, what they were planning to do in Paris. 'Only staying two days,' he said briskly. 'Collect the pension, dismantle the sewing machine, hit the road again.' They were bringing the machine to a young granddaughter in Vienna, who was to be set up in the sewing business. 'Give us three years,' he said, 'and we'll show you a new Yugoslavia.'

I wondered how many natives, in Austria or anywhere else, had any idea of the industry and energy foreigners use in order to keep several families going, in two countries. And I was instantly reminded of a woman on an Irish bus last year, who had only uttered one sentence as various foreigners boarded the bus in Navan: 'Too many of them foreign nationalists here now,' she said. And I knew it was something she'd heard somewhere, not something she really believed herself.

A HANDY TOOL

Berni Dwan

Berni Dwan is a freelance journalist, writing mainly about technology and science for national and international publications. She lives in Dublin with her husband, Brian, and her daughter, Hannah.

How often have we praised someone's handiwork? It could be a fine painting, a patchwork quilt, the way they play Chopin's études or the way they wield a sword. Aristotle praised the hand as 'the instrument for instruments'. The hand that holds the pen, the paintbrush, the tennis racquet, the surgical instruments, the hoe, the steering-wheel or the reigns of a horse. The hand that touches the keys of a piano, the keys of a computer keyboard or the Braille symbols in a book. Aristotle considered the hand and the intellect as the 'two inner instruments with which we use outer instruments'.

It is not simply a matter of what we can do with our hands. More importantly, it is what we can do with all the instruments we can grasp in our hands and the way the brain and the hand interact to complete the task. From earliest times, the mechanism of the hand was seen as perfectly designed for grasping or apprehension, and isn't it interesting that apprehension in both Latin and English assumed the dual meaning of physically grasping something or intellectually grasping a new concept or idea?

Just like the faculty of reason separates the human from the animal mind, the opposing thumb separates the human hand from its animal counterpart. Indeed, Aristotle was of the opinion that 'man received hands because he *was* the most intelligent'. 'Nature,' he said, 'like an intelligent person, always distributes instruments according to the recipient's ability to use them.' Luckily for us, nature in her wisdom decided that we humans *were* the most suitable recipients. You wouldn't give an elephant a violin then, not only because it wouldn't have the hands to play it, but more importantly because it would not have the intellectual capacity to handle anything as adaptable as the human hand. It would, metaphorically speaking, be 'all fingers and thumbs'.

In his *Ecclesiastical History of the English People*, the venerable Bede described a system of finger numerals for I to 9,999. The middle, ring and little fingers of the left hand were single digits, while the thumb and index fingers counted in tens. The thumb and index finger on the right hand counted in hundreds, while the middle, ring and little fingers counted in thousands. He then described the finger gymnastics required for saying a number. I failed on 'I' because it requires bending the little finger into the middle joint of the palm. Trying to do this without bending the ring finger also is impossible and makes me marvel all the more at those who are highly proficient in sign language. From 10,000 onwards it gets easier, as only gestures are needed. If, for example, you won the eighth-century equivalent of *Who Wants to Be a Millionaire* you would have expressed that million by clasping both hands together over your head with the fingers interlaced. And it didn't stop at mere counting. Bede also explained how the nineteen joints and nails in the left hand or the twenty-eight joints in both hands could be used to memorise the lunar and solar cycles respectively.

Aristotle grasped the hammer firmly and hit the nail accurately on the head when he observed that the hand is 'a claw, a hoof, a horn, a spear, a sword, and any other weapon or instrument whatever'.

Some years previously, I had made a documentary about Coole and Lady Gregory. I illustrated it with excerpts from Anne Gregory's delightful book on her childhood at Coole – *Me and Nu*. The 'Nu' was her sister Catherine, who as a child thought 'Nu' was her name – 'Anne, you do this and Richard, you do that and you help your sister.' The thought occurred to me – I wonder are Anne and Catherine still alive and, if so, wouldn't it be wonderful to bring them back to Coole to re-live and record all those memories. Well, yes, they were very much alive (Anne in Devon, Catherine in County Cork) and, yes, they would love to come back to Coole. And so it happened in September 1994.

I wasn't the first John Quinn in their lives of course. There was John Quinn the Irish American lawyer, who had a 'dalliance' with their grandmother and who sent them a box of apples every Christmas. It seemed entirely appropriate that I continue the tradition, so when I met the two ladies in Gort, I presented them with a bag of Tesco apples. Ninety-nine pence – hang the expense, RTÉ were footing the bill.

There followed two days of magic as the stories tumbled from the two ladies' collective memory. We walked through the woods of Coole Park in the rain, visited their summer home in the Burren and their grandmother's home in Galway City. The memories of Mr Yeats, who went around humming all the time and who claimed he had petted a badger in the woods when it was really their terrier dog ... Of Mr O'Casey who, when asked to carve his initials on the autograph tree, found it no trouble at all – hadn't he often carved them on the door of his tenement at home in Dublin (and what on earth was a tenement, the children wondered). Anne and Catherine's childhood was truly idyllic, permeated by the presence of their remarkable grandmother. She always found time for them – she might be writing a play, busy negotiating the return of the Lane Pictures or simply overseeing the running of Coole Estate, but she found time for 'me and Nu' when they would burst in to tell her of their daily adventures in the woods of Coole.

And, of course, they would need provisions for their daily adventures. So they would go to the orchard and stock up with apples. How to carry them? Simply stuff them in the legs of their knee-length knickers ... Seventy years on, Anne Gregory recalls with glee the day they met their mother and August John in the garden. Mother wanted to know why the children were waddling along – and so they had to shamefacedly unload the apples while Augustus John fell about the place laughing.

Memories of their beloved George Bernard Shaw, who cheated them at 'hunt the thimble' and who wrote a special poem to them – 'Two Ladies of Galway' – on the back of five postcards. Two remarkable ladies with remarkable stories. Our journey ends in Galway in the house where they learned of their father's death as an Irish airman in the First World War. They remember a huge stuffed bear on the stairs. 'A bit like you,' Catherine says to me, 'not as much hair as you of course.' Before we part, I ask Anne to sign my copy of her book, which she does with grace and typical impish humour. *Dear J.Q., thank you for the apples – pity we couldn't carry them as in olden days ...*

CHRISTMAS 1987

Anthony Jordan

Anthony Jordan, a native of Ballyhaunis, now lives in Dublin. He has written biographies of Major John MacBride, Sean MacBride, Conor Cruise O'Brien, Winston Churchill, Christy Brown and, most recently, a critical biography of W.B. Yeats.

I have had a haven of privacy I can repair to for the last thirty years. It is not a place, but rather a person I briefly knew. There, anywhere, I am alone with her: we are alone as we once were, alone amid a crowd of people going about their work. In a way, I feel myself vulnerable to her presence and yet I welcome it. I would not change it even if I could; I welcome it, I welcome her. She is a refuge for me. In times of intense happiness I seek her most. I want to include her in the ecstasy, though knowing that cannot be. It is painful too, very painful, and the tears will flow on my cheeks. I remember the letters I wrote to her, the hopes expressed, the promises, the lack of bargaining, the acceptance of whatever materialised. She was mine; I saw her struggling; I saw her pain; I felt my own pain. And whether paradoxical or not, pain does purify; it scours the soul as well as the body.

I disputed with a good Bishop once, on her behalf. I told him that his theology was mistaken, that he was ignorant of the reality that enveloped her.

And so I revisit her quite regularly during all these years, often by choice, but sometimes out of necessity. Always the tears cleanse me as a douche when I think of what might have been and what was. Though she passed me by in a flash she, like nothing else, has given me a means to repair, recover, recuperate in, a painful interlude which I would not trade because it brings us together until the next time. Oliver Gogarty wrote in his poem 'Golden Stockings' how he stored up in his memory many thoughts that would last if he were blinded. My thoughts of one particular visitation on Christmas Eve some years ago went like this.

Christmas 1987

The stars shine brightly on this cool Christmas night.
A red candle flames from our window.
I wave to my wife and daughter as they pass to Midnight Mass.
A white stocking hangs limply, a young girl sleeps expectantly.

Happiness wells within me, unwished for, unwanted.
So soon, by thought of you, my first born,
My cross, my joy, the swell is overtaken.
Thrice I saw you, yet you are the measure of all I am.

The eyes fill; the tears fall on my cheeks.
It is a sacrament I receive from you.
My girl in the incubator, who was not there when last I called.
But removed, transferred to a cold loose wet clay,
In a wooden shoebox, beneath a tree, beside a stony path,
In nineteen seventy.

KATE'S MOTHER

Rita Ann Higgins

Rita Ann Higgins has published several
collections, including *An Awful Racket* and
Sunny Side Plucked: New & Selected Poems. The
Selected Poems was awarded a Poetry Society
recommendation

Kate's mother had a psychiatric
illness, but it was easier all round
not to mention anything that sounded
remotely like mental. The euphemisms
generally used were 'mammy isn't well',
or 'mammy is poorly', or 'mammy isn't
herself this weather'.

Mammy wasn't herself for a long
time as far as Kate was concerned. Kate
was a carer. She got a carer's allowance,
it was her job to care. It was her job to
cope. After all wasn't she being paid to
do so? She had her own family as well,
Seán and the four children. But looking after her mother took most of her
time and energy.

About five years ago her mother
started to go funny in the head. She

was getting directives from the FBI and Rome. Kate used to tell her to give up that nonsense. At first it was a hoot hearing about what the voices said to her that morning or how she had to meet the president of the high court in the afternoon. Still Kate was getting tired. Seán and the children were missing her only half being there. Kate was his wife and their mother. In bed she was too exhausted to respond to his sexual advances. With the children she was contrary, she tended to fly off the handle for the least little thing. She was there but she wasn't with them.

Over the years, the voices from the mother began wearing Kate down, they were getting louder. Kate was quietly and calmly having her own personal breakdown. The family wouldn't entertain this at all. No carer of ours is going to crack up, no way Jóse. Kate was a carer, she always cared for other people, even when the government didn't give her a derisory sum to do so. And once a carer … It was ridiculous Kate having a breakdown; it wasn't just ridiculous, they weren't having it. No carer of ours is having a breakdown. There'll be no breakdown on our watch, baby. Only it was always her watch.

Seán told her in no uncertain terms that he'd put up with her neglect for long enough while she was waiting hand and foot on her mother. He told her to stop her carry on, bursting into tears at the breakfast table and spreading despair and gloom all over the house with the fears she was collecting. She was afraid what the postman might bring. She was afraid of the Angelus on the telly, she was afraid of the wind in the trees. She was afraid.

Seán was loosing patience with the coper. 'For crying out loud', he'd say, 'what's wrong with you, you can't even go out the back for a bucket of coal? Last year I saw you hauling a bag of it over the back fence.'

Kate no longer knew what cope meant. It was only a word that was used a lot in the house. It seemed to her to be a very heavy word. A word loaded with stones and it was resting on her shoulders. When she stood up cope made her stoop. When she tried to walk she stumbled with cope. When Kate's mother slipped in the hall and broke her hip, Kate ran clean out of cope.

WRITER-IN-
RESIDENCE

Carlo Gébler

Carlo Gébler was born in Dublin in 1954,
brought up in London and now lives
outside Enniskillen, Co. Fermanagh. The
author of several novels and plays and a
member of Aósdána, he is writer-in-
residence in HM Prison, Maghaberry.

Because I am a writer in my real life
outside the prison gate, I obviously
believe in literature. Therefore, it isn't
exactly hard work spending one day a
week in HM Prison, Maghaberry as
writer-in-residence, trying to help
prisoners to write.

I also believe it's good for me. I
need to be in the world. If I wasn't
working in the jail I hope I'd be
working for the Samaritans one
evening a week.

Because I'm in the jail regularly, I
have also occasionally been able to do

something I felt proud of. One episode stands out. It didn't involve literature.

Crossing the circle one day, I noticed a prisoner on a chair on the other side of the grille. He was obviously new because he was sobbing and shaking.

The officer let me through the grille and locked it behind. I touched him on the shoulder and he looked up. I asked what the matter was. He explained he'd gone to court that morning with his wife. He'd expected a huge fine. Instead, he'd got a custodial sentence. His wife had collapsed and he had been brought to jail. He had never been to jail before. He was terrified. He feared assault or rape.

I asked him why he was sitting at the grille. He said he was hoping the MO would come. He wanted something to put him to sleep.

I told him frankly there was little likelihood of him being assaulted. I couldn't pretend these sorts of things didn't happen. But, I pointed out to him, which was true, all the assaults I'd heard of during all the years I'd been working in the jail had been by prisoners on other prisoners they knew. I'd not heard of new prisoners being attacked.

'I could be wrong,' I added, 'but I've never heard of it.'

He asked me what I did. I told him. We started talking. I didn't ask why he was there. I guessed he'd killed someone when he was driving. I talked instead about what to do. I told him not to accept cigarettes, not to accept favours and to talk only when spoken to and otherwise to keep quiet. If he was harassed he was to go the officers and tell them. He would either be locked in his cell or moved.

This was not earth-shattering advice. Nonetheless, after about twenty minutes he stopped crying and said, 'You're the first person not connected to the courts or the police or the prison that's spoken to me today.'

'What don't we walk up to your cell?' I said.

He shook his head. He was determined to wait for the MO

But he was going to be all right now, he assured me. Really, he said. He was emphatic.

We shook hands. I went up on the wing. I never saw him again.

I tell this story not because I did something special or remarkable. I didn't. I did what anyone would have done. I just stopped and talked for a while. It made a difference to the prisoner – I really believe that – but anyone could have made that difference. I just happened to be the person who happened to walk by.

The real point of the story is that it pinpoints what it is we who teach in the jail are really there to do. Of course we are there to teach. But over and above this we have a more important duty. We are there to be human. As long as that is how we are, then there always is a chance that sometimes we can do right.

THE POOLS
WINNER

Sam McAughtry

Sam McAughtry, author, broadcaster, jour-
nalist and trade unionist, has published nine
books. He was Columnist of Year with *The
Irish Times* in 1986, a member of Seanad
Éireann 1996–9 and received an Honorary
Doctorate, NUI Maynooth, 1998.

In our district there used to be a
newsagent's and post office run by a
man who had lost his right arm when
he was young. He was in his late fifties,
his name was Mister Bryson and he
was greatly respected by the whole
neighbourhood. He dressed well in
good quality tweeds, the best of shirts
and hand-made shoes and he could
converse with the customers on all
levels as he was handing them their
papers, magazines or stamps. The
teachers from the nearby school and
the doctors and dentists all bought

their papers from him, as did the working-class people who lived in the streets around, and Mister Bryson loved to talk to them about current events. Everybody had respect for him because he was interesting over and above his general knowledge: he was a great swimmer and diver, never mind the one arm, and he could write with the left hand, tie his shoe laces and even cut the hedge outside with one arm and strategically placed straps.

In our local, Jim Douglas, who lived beside me and was a foreman in a big factory, mentioned two things to me one evening. One was that he had won big money on the pools that very week and the other was that he would dearly love to buy the shop from Mister Bryson. 'I love the way he gets respect,' he said, 'that's through meeting the people. When you own a respectable shop you get respect. Mister Bryson's important, more so than somebody working in a factory, like me.'

'But sure you're a foreman,' I said. 'Doesn't that get you respect?' He shook his head. 'Only from the workers,' he replied, 'and they have to be respectful. I would love to have the kind of broad respect that Mister Bryson has.'

Well, he made an approach to Mister Bryson and surprisingly his bid was well received. It seems that Mister Bryson wanted a break from the early-morning aspect of running a newsagent's. One Monday morning, instead of Mister Bryson, Jim Douglas appeared, smiling, behind the counter.

I wished him luck when I bought my paper, but there was a bit of an exchange before me between Jim and one of the teachers that made me think.

'I see where Ulster has let itself down again,' he said.

'Oh,' said the teacher, a pleasant enough lady, 'and how's that?'

'The Aga Khan's horse was down to run at Downpatrick, but it was stabbed in Killyleagh in the stable.' Jim pointed the item out in the *Belfast News Letter* and the teacher peered at it.

'It wasn't stabbed at Killyleagh,' she said, frowning. 'It was stabled at Killyleagh.' Then she walked out.

On top of that sort of handicap, Jim ran into the worst kind of problem for a shopkeeper — the working-class neighbours knew him too well. Although he was a harmless, gentle enough soul, they took their custom elsewhere because he was one of their own, acting as if he were Mister Bryson, all dressed up, only Jim looked as if he was going to a funeral instead of running a shop, looking uncomfortable in his spanking new navy serge suit and brown shoes. His money was pools money and therefore not to be respected. Right from the start the project was doomed. The professional people weren't interested in Jim's references to the local soccer team, Crusaders, or the upcoming final of the darts pairs championship in the local pub. God help him, after a year he had to sell at a loss and go back to the factory, reduced to working on the bench.

'I just don't understand people,' he said to me in the local. That was the way he put it. I remember thinking that, after his experience, never mind understanding people, he should have been able to give public lectures on the subject.

MY FATHER'S LEGACY

Geraldine Mills

Geraldine Mills writes poetry and short
stories and has won many awards for her
work, including the Hennessy/*Tribune*
New Irish Writer Award in 2000. She has
published two collections of poetry,
Unearthing Your Own and *Toil the Dark Harvest*.

A Jew's harp, a honey-coloured
moneybag and a cobbler's last
were the main items of my father's
legacy when he died. He had little else
to leave apart from a faded photograph
of him taken with my sister and me at
the station, that was miles along the
platform in my child mind. The green
and cream of my coat's collar, the
angora cap around my younger sister's
face, pressed to his rasp of skin in the
tiny booth.

There are memories of scraps of
letters on blue-lined Basildon bond
that he wrote to his angels as he called

us; posted from some Paddy place in London after the sweat of the building site was washed away in the cold drip of shower of a silent bed-sit. Strained images of him arriving in Galway with his dark curly hair, a large man in a worn donkey jacket. We sat and watched him clear a plate of eggs and bread fried golden on the crisp of rashers. He let us dip our own bread into the golden yolk of egg. He died when I was ten.

On those twice-yearly visits home, Christmas and summertime, the golden moneybag jangled, the Jew's harp taken from the mantelpiece filled the room with its twang before he drew us in line with our shoes: my brown leather lace-ups, my sister's black ones with the T-strap, my mother's high heels, his own large good ones. He sat, his left leg over his right, the shoemaker's last resting in the bowl of his lap. On the bench beside him, the strips of leather, the heels of rubber. Then with awl and hammer he got to work. He stitched the place where a growing foot burst its sides, repaired, replaced the button heel of my mother's, the wide pocket of his own. Made good another wearing.

There is a twang of the Jew's harp half-remembered, the silence of the moneybag long emptied. The cobbler's last is all that's left of him, thrown into the back of memory until my daughter starts tap-dancing classes and her shoes demand heel taps. I unearth the rusted manx shape of heels and toes from the shed's rattlebag of tools. I dare carry out what he did when he came home, those rare occasions, upending sole, slipping the black leather heel to heel on the last. Nestle it in my lap.

I take the hammer and get to work, holding a half-dozen tacks at the edge of my mouth as he did. Pin the felt cushion in place. Position the bright metal tap in the shape of the heel. The sound of the hammer strikes the tacks and he is back with us, paring, piercing, tip, tapping to drive the final nail home.

My daughter slips on the shoes, breaks the silence of the wooden boards, hears the sound in her feet. She taps, riffs and time steps across the floor. Ginger Rogers, Fred Astaire, Bojangles. Straining to mark the timbers of stage floors from Galway to the edge of her dreams.

anybody else, just me and him. We cycled up the back road and when we got to the church there were but a few silent souls, or sinners, like ourselves in the pews. It was on one of those dark silent mornings I first viewed the immensity of a starry sky. My father leaned the bike against the high wall of the Christian Brothers' school. He stood me on the handlebars. 'Look up,' he said and I looked. He traced then for me the outline of the Plough and of the warrior, Orion. He showed me the Milky Way. I stared. It was dark but there were seas of great light in the sky. I swam in some enormous depths. The flinty stoned pebble-dash of the Christian Brother's wall glinted and so too did the frost on the grass.

It sometimes frightens me looking up there, I heard my father say from below. So immense.

Was I frightened? Not on my father's handlebars, I wasn't. Not with his arms holding me. My father wouldn't let me fall. And didn't the mysterious music of the stars follow me and hum through the high rafters in our church? Wasn't it all heavenly and religious?

I did not know then how all the years would pass: the day when I was eight that my father refereed the rugby match between his old Alma Mater and the local team of Templemore might have been the paradigm for all those passing years. The field was behind the same church. He blew on a garda whistle and I think what must have happened was that both sides had enough of his blowing. Once he disappeared beneath the scrum of men, and when he reappeared again he was black and bloodied and kicked and beaten. I was pleased to see him but disappointed both teams should have turned against him. I did not think much of the job of referee. Many times during the course of his life I would see him similarly rewarded.

I did not know then, either, that there would be an end. But it did come. He was dying in the hospice and it was my night to stay up with him. Distressed, he asked me to take him down the corridor to the toilet. Again and again he asked me and again and again I lifted him in my arms and took him, for he was deeply agitated.

That was seventeen years ago. A night, I later thought, on which I carried out a chore most lacking in significance. Most mundane. A night, I thought, I might have done more. Maybe I should have lifted him to the window. Maybe I should have shown him the stars he once showed me. But I don't think there was a window anyway. And maybe there were no stars on that night. It was a dark corridor. I did carry him to where he asked to be taken to, carried him as far as I could take him, that time a few hours before he died. But it was most mundane. What did he say to me? 'Don't let me fall,' he said. 'I'm afraid you're going to let me fall.'

GUILLEMOTS

Theodore Deppe

Theodore Deppe is the author of three
books of poetry. His most recent collection
is *Cape Clear: New and Selected Poems*.

When my sister learned she had
breast cancer, she phoned our
mother and got an unexpected
response. Mother laughed. She wasn't
being cruel. It turned out that she'd
been diagnosed with breast cancer that
same day.

I received the news on a mobile
phone on Cape Clear Island, three
thousand miles from home. It took me
a while to be able to really hear the
words. I walked to South Harbour,
listening instead to the cries of the
oystercatchers as they skimmed across
the water.

While I was walking, I noticed
several guillemots struggling along the

beach. Small waves propelled them onto the rocks, and before they could right themselves, they were sucked back with the water's retreat. These black and white seabirds were covered with a film of oil. I couldn't see any slick along the shore, but somewhere out at sea there'd been a spill.

A friend helped me catch four of them: we flung our coats over the birds, then carried them to the house to wash off the oil. The birds nipped our fingers until we learned to hold them by the back of the head. As we scrubbed the petroleum from their feathers, we also were washing off the body oils that protect them from the cold. After we'd finished bathing them, my friend suggested we blow-dry the guillemots to keep them warm. To my surprise, the birds loved the blow dryer, spreading their wings out to dry. They even rubbed up against the nozzle, basking in the heat.

For weeks we sliced bits of herring and hand-fed the guillemots. I became so obsessed with the birds that my wife took me aside and told me something obvious: 'The guillemots aren't your mother or your sister.' Islanders told us that once the birds were ill enough to be caught, they'd already ingested too much poison to survive. Sure enough, the guillemots stopped eating and died, until only one was left. My friend set up a mirror in the pen so that it wouldn't get lonely. It haunted that mirror, longing for the world of sea birds and the sea.

Which guillemot, I wondered, was not my mother or sister? The ones that died or the one that we released back into the wild on Christmas Eve? I had no idea if the bird would make it through the harsh winter, but I'm glad we gave it a chance. And I hope that back in the States, the doctors and nurses who are taking care of my family are confused in the same way that I was. 'Yes,' I want to tell each of them, 'those women you are taking care of are your mother, your sister. You can't promise to pull them through, but remember, they are your mother, your sister.'

RULE OF THUMB

Celia de Fréine

Celia de Fréine is a poet, playwright and screenwriter who writes in Irish and English. Her collection of poetry *Fiacha Fola* has been awarded Gradam Litríochta Chló Iar-Chonnachta 2004.

Each summer, as a child, I used to travel from Dublin to a seaside village in the North of Ireland, where I'd stay with my granny. One year a girl the same age as myself, Hester, appeared in a small cottage across the street. We became friends straight away.

Hester belonged to a strict religious sect who had to attend three prayer meetings on Sunday, a day on which her family were allowed do nothing else, not even cook a meal. The swimming pool was out of bounds, as were the tennis courts and cinema, but because we were such good friends, I was prepared to swim with Hester in the crab-infested sea and play singles on the uneven pavement down by the gasometer.

My aunt was getting married this particular summer. Neighbours and friends came from all over bearing gifts. One evening, Hester's father arrived with some glassware. My aunt invited him into the parlour.

'How about a wee drop of sherry?' she asked.

I watched in horror as the amber liquid disappeared down his throat. What would Hester say? Her attitude the following morning surprised me. While members of the sect were forbidden to drink alcohol, it wasn't polite to refuse what was offered when visiting someone else's home.

The day of the wedding approached. I was to be a flower girl and had had a dress tailor-made. But my main worry was not about the ceremony itself, or the reception afterwards, but when would it end? Would I be back in time to catch the tide for my swim with Hester?

As soon as the hired car spewed me out at my granny's door, I was up the stairs and changed. Clutching my togs, I shot over to Hester's. Her mother opened the door and brought me into the cottage. Inside everything was grey – the floor, the walls, the curtains. She explained that I could no longer play with Hester. Hester had been given special permission by her church to play with me until now, only because no one from her own religion lived nearby. This was about to change. A young girl, one of their own, had moved in around the corner. Hester would have to play with her from now on.

I made my way down to the sea. Some local women who swam every day were already in the water. They beckoned me to join them. I should have been thrilled at being accepted into their company, but my mind was on Hester, on how her family could end our friendship and on how we could do nothing about it. Bending the rules, imbibing the odd glass of sherry, was one thing, but to defy openly their religious leaders would be out of the question.

I never saw her again. When I went back the following year, the grey cottage had been sold. I often think of our friendship and of the girl I was that summer. The feelings of disappointment and disbelief I experienced then go a small way towards understanding the terror and bewilderment I see in news reports today, on the faces of children, here and abroad, who are victims of religious or ethnic hostility.

SISTER

Tony Flannery

Tony Flannery is a native of Attymon, Co. Galway. He is a priest with the Redemptorists and has written widely on both religious and secular topics.

I can see the goose!' These words were spoken by my sister, whom I never knew. She died, at the age of three, a few years before I was born. It was back in the forties. The war was still on and neither medical help nor transport was freely available. My mother always asserted that she should not have died; that it was a simple problem she had, if the right medicine had been available at the right time. And the fact that she was her first born surely made her special in my mother's eyes.

When she was dying, a few years ago, at the age of ninety, my mother talked a lot about that first child. She mostly told simple, everyday stories from those years, recalling them with a vividness that contrasted with her dramatic loss of memory about recent events and people. The story of the missing goose, and how the little child had come running in to tell her that he had been found, was one of them.

But not all the conundrums that faced her in those last days were as easily solved as the goose. Though she spent much of the time dwelling in the past, she had her lucid moments. And they were dangerous times for me, sitting by the bed. She was, in a sense, gazing into eternity, into that mist that surrounds our death, and trying to lift the veil.

'Tell me,' she said suddenly one day, after a long period of rambling in her youth, 'do you believe in the next life?'

I had resolved that I would try to speak truthfully, that I would resist the temptation to give simple answers to difficult questions.

'I think so,' I replied.

'What will it be like?'

I did not answer this for a long time and I could feel her eyes boring into me. I knew it was important to her.

'You should know,' she said, 'after all you are a priest.'

'I don't,' I said. 'I believe that it will be good; that it will surpass all our expectations. But beyond that, I know nothing.'

This time the long silence was from her and I wondered had her mind once again drifted off. I almost hoped it had. She had become such a tiny woman, sitting up in the big bed, wondering what was ahead of her. It seemed too big a question for someone so frail and old. I anxiously searched her face for signs of fear. To my relief I couldn't find any. Just a wonderment.

'It is such a puzzle,' she said. 'Some day I must sit down and try to work it all out.' And with that she settled back onto the pillow and closed her eyes.

Ninety years in this world and the puzzle remained. She went into eternity a few days later, still with that sense of wonderment, still not knowing what was ahead of her. But, as far as I could see, she was not afraid. She trusted. Whatever awaited her, she would embrace it as she had embraced life. And she believed it would embrace her and welcome her. Maybe that is as much as any of us can do in the face of death. Maybe it is enough.

LITTLE MAN

Conor O'Callaghan

Conor O'Callaghan has published two
collections of poetry and one book of
prose non-fiction, *Red Mist — Roy Keane and
the Football Civil War.*

Last week it was 'actually'. Last week
everything was actually this and
actually that. This week it is
'ridiculous', said with a big twinkle in
his eye and pronounced as if it were a
perfect rhyme for 'Nicholas'. He thinks
it is ridiculous that he should be
expected to eat all his Weetabix. He
thinks the lollypop lady on our way to
school is ridiculous. He thinks staying
in school until three o'clock, and not
half past twelve as it was before
Christmas, is ridiculous. He thinks the
noise his father makes when he sings
along with the radio is ridiculous. Just
last night I heard him chatting in the

bed as late as half past nine. When I went up and asked him what the matter was, he said he thought going to sleep was ridiculous.

Our son is four. He seems to have it in his head that four is when you come of age. He has already taken to beginning sentences with phrases like 'When I was a small boy' or 'Now that I'm big'. He seems to have it in his head that four is the age of consent – the time of life when you get the key to the door. He thinks he should be allowed to come out playing snooker with me and his uncle on Tuesday nights. He really believes that he could manage the car – if only his parents would let him. The odd evening when he and his sister are feeling giddy, he stands in the hall in his pyjamas and my jacket and boots and calls back to us in the kitchen: 'I'm away out for a point of Guinness.' Since turning four he has become philosophical. He has begun to ask awkward questions, although about nothing so trivial as the birds and the bees. Umpteen times now we have found ourselves sitting there nodding at each other, as if to say, 'It's your turn to answer the unanswerable.' He wants to know what it means to be old. He wants to know why dolls don't die. He wonders why the sky is blue. His mother goes for the truth. Once I stepped into the kitchen to find that she had arranged soggy pears and kiwis into a DIY solar system. He was sitting on the sideline with binoculars and a stethoscope, looking as if he regretted asking where the sun goes at night. Later, I told him that two men go up every night and carry the sun down in a net hung between their separate helicopters. I told him that they keep the sun in a big shed in a small coastal village three miles from were we live and that they clean it once a week. He prefers my stories, but I think he believes his mother.

Since starting school he has become conscious of his appearance in a way that he never was before. It used to be that the morning after we gave him a bath, he would wake up with his hair standing on end, looking as if he had been struck by lightning in his dreams – and it didn't bother him in the slightest.

Then, one of the other boys at school said something about his hair to his best friend Desmond, and then Desmond said it back to him. Now, he insists on wearing a baseball cap while eating his breakfast. Time and again I am struck by how strange the day-to-day life of a four-year-old is. When he was teething – a couple of years ago – he used to soothe his aching gums by chewing a Volkswagen Beetle. Nowadays he takes a Wagon Wheel for his break and he alternates between an alien (with alien babies) and a penguin for company. He keeps the shaft of a plastic golf club beside his bed and calls it a 'gun'. He drifts off every night to the sound of my grandmother's music box, unwinding through 'The Isle of Capri'. And he thinks you don't die until you're ninety-nine.

In ten years from now he will spend his summers sleeping in until two in the afternoon and shaving twice a day. He will beg for money from us and accuse us of never loving him – all in the same breath. So, for the time being, I'm inclined just to enjoy him being my little man. And I have begun to realise that four is probably as good as it gets.

BELL

Mary P. Wilkinson

Mary P. Wilkinson lives in Co. Galway. Her
writing has featured in various publications
and on RTÉ. She won first prize in The
Original Competition, Listowel 2004.

For two days you've been sick, my
little one. When at first the spots
appeared they formed small clusters,
tiny maps of countries, random
speckles of red that gradually grew to
cover your skin. Now they are like large
continents flowing into one another
until a massive fiery planet covers your
body, your face. You are submerged by
illness.

Just two days ago I hunted down a
doctor and struggled through the June
throng in a golden setting sun seeking
our salvation, clasping a piece of paper
with a formula scribbled on it for you.
'I don't like giving him antibiotics,' I

said, but the pharmacist just looked and said dismissively, 'Your child is very sick.' Now I spoon something into you that I can't even pronounce and tell you, Mmm mint, thick creamy mint. You take it. Trusting. Anxious. Obedient. Your furnace burns on. I feel your forehead by running my lips back and forth against your skin. It burns. It cools. It burns again. Fluctuation. Degeneration. Denigration. I think about the lofty conversations I had about immunisation. About choice. How definite I was. How right. 'For sure, it's all about choice,' I said, aloud, right there in front of you, small man.

Poor baby. I stand in the doorway and watch. You sit on the couch in the afternoon. The curtains block out the sunshine. Outside the thud of your brother's basketball is audible. You seem hunched over, almost a hundred years old, wrapped in a blanked I bought in Mexico.

Oh, it was a long time ago when I walked back across the bridge spanning the Rio Grande after a day's outing. My face, one in a sea of people. The novelty of it! Souvenirs. I had that blanket, a bottle of Cuervo Gold and a bell. A clay bell. How can a bell be made of clay? Bells should be light, glassy, airy things. It must have been the bird, a dove, engraved into the surface that caught my eye. Attracted me to it. Soaring upward towards the sky. Some poor soul must have made it, in the back room of a miserable little shop, and yet, at the time all I could think about was how primitive and authentic my clay bell was, how good it would look in my home. And so, for a few pesetas, a bargain!

The river ran fast that day, little man. It swirled and eddied under the gridded bridge and threw brown froth all along its bank. The two boys below were a little older than you, though not by much. I watched them as they clambered aboard the makeshift raft, their brown flawless skin wet from the water, their feet bare. I saw a man directing them, beckoning, urging them onto the small boat.

I wanted to call out to them, 'Where's your mother, what

about your mother?' But I stayed silent, pushed along by the steady stream of people with their piñatas and ponchos and tequilas. If they had crossed the river to the other side there would have been the barbed wire, long coils of spiked wire that would surely have torn into their sallow skin. Stopping them. Immigration. Immunisation. Humanisation. All words.

There, my small pustulated child, it's time to sleep. Hush now. I'll find that bell. I know it's stowed away, perhaps lying silent in the attic. I'll find it and take it out and hang it in the window and we'll listen for its gentle tinkle of clay and we'll let it ring its ringing over and over and over again.

A LIFE LIVED

Nicola Lindsay

Nicola Lindsay's published work includes a children's book and a collection of her poetry. The author of four published novels, with a fifth due in 2005, her work has been broadcast and anthologised both in Ireland and England.

When my mother was young, she was fiery. She sometimes shouted, banged doors and occasionally, when really roused, she threw things. My dad grew skilled at ducking and side-stepping. I can still see the slow-motion drip of a lobbed saucepan full of Irish stew slipping down the wall onto the floor. The carrots — little constellations of orange in the brown — glistened as they slid earthwards to join the chunks of meat at the feet of our surprised but appreciative dog.

The other side of her nature was

affectionate and fun-loving and we all had our full share of hugs and cuddles. In many households back then it was not considered the 'done thing' to articulate one's feelings or be demonstrative, but our mother was somewhat Mediterranean in her behaviour. It showed in her love of Italian clothes and in her cooking and it was evident in the way she read avidly in French and Italian.

At the age of twenty-one I left home and never lived in England again. My mother and I came together briefly and irregularly and often, after spending a few days together, somewhat uncomfortably. We could upset each other very easily and frequently did. It was with relief that I would depart from the family home back to my own life: my home, my children, my garden, my way of doing things.

Then, when she was only sixty-eight, my mother became very ill with a heart problem. It was necessary for her to have a quadruple by-pass. We knew that the young woman who'd lived not far from my mother had had the same operation the previous month. She died on the operating table. Suddenly, all the misunderstandings, jealousies and irritations were unimportant and forgotten.

She must have felt frightened as the day approached, but she appeared calm and self-possessed. Unable to be with her, we spoke on the phone a few hours before she went down to the operating theatre. It was she who reassured me that all would be well.

And it was. My mother lived for eleven more years, ten of which had a quality of life that was excellent. In the last year, though, she became frail and each time I met her at the airport my heart would lurch. Each time we parted I feared for her, hating leaving her as she stood beside my brother, smiling and waving, seeming smaller and somehow insubstantial, as if the slightest jolt from a careless passer-by would knock her over. At each parting I wanted to rush back and give her one more last hug.

When she died, suddenly, without any warning, I tried to

cheer myself with the thought that she hadn't wanted to become any more dependent, that the final year had been hard for her to live through. I thought of how serene she had become in that last year, how we spent time together quietly enjoying each other's company, how we hadn't argued or become irritated. And that is how I will think of her: patient, affectionate, amused by life's absurdities and blessed with a tranquillity that I don't remember her having when I was growing up.

HOLLY

Peter Cunningham

Peter Cunningham's *Monument* novels, based in Waterford where he grew up, have received wide critical acclaim. His best-selling novel, *The Taoiseach*, first published in 2003, is based on Irish politics during the period 1965–91.

My grandfather was the county doctor. He was a mighty handsome man if my old photographs tell the truth. He went out in his trap in all weathers to Baiscne and to Deilt, to Irrus and Eillne, even to Sibrille by the sea.

The truth is, he wasn't, of course. One of my grandfathers was a pig dealer and the other was a professional gambler; but I had spent my first eight years living in the house of a man who had once been the county doctor for that part of Waterford and so it was to him I turned for the opening lines of my novel *Consequences of the Heart*.

Fiction is like that. You have what you have, locked away somewhere in your head, and one day you use it. In this case the house, called Inchera, had a distant view over the Atlantic in Tramore and the doctor, a Dr Stephenson, had died, I think, sometime in the 1920s. My mother's stepfather bought the house and my mother went to live there. After the war she married my father and he moved in.

Dr Stephenson had indeed travelled the county lanes in a pony and trap and he had, like my Dr Church in *Consequences of the Heart*, delivered babies, *closed the tired old eyes of the dead*, and *thrown open the windows of cottages to the long ostracised air*. I know these things because his son, William, told me them.

William had grown up in the same house as I and smelled the same sea and heard the same seagulls, or their ancestors. When he was sixteen he decided to become a Jesuit. This was around 1905. On his last day in Inchera his father suggested a picnic. The pair set out in the pony and trap around the lake called Knockaderry. It was May and there was heat in the grass and new ferns. Father and son chatted about life, about the future, about the fact that William was going away. They got back into the trap to go home, but William suddenly leaped out again and ran to a wild holly sapling and pulled it up by its roots. When he told his father he was bringing it home to plant it, Dr Stephenson had laughed.

'It'll never grow,' he said, 'Never.'

When I was a child and William was already an old man, he came back every year to Tramore and stayed in a guesthouse for a fortnight. In the span of time since the day of his last picnic he had lived in Sydney, a place he still described as a frontier town, and in the Channel Islands, where he had become friends with the famous Jesuit philosopher Tailhard de Chardin. William himself had written a number of books — simple mediations on prayer.

After mass each morning in Tramore during his summer

holidays, he walked down the Priest's Road to Inchera. In the early days I was always playing in the garden that went around the house. My favourite place was my swing. William Stephenson used to laugh as he pushed me on it. The swing hung by two ropes from a stout bough of his holly tree.

NIGHT-TIME IN THE SIMON COMMUNITY

by Seán Ó Riain

Seán Ó Riain, born in Cork in 1940 and a
former secondary teacher, has been writing
in Irish and English since 1964. He is the
author of three books, *Roman Life and Literature*, *Seal le Síomón* and *Solidarity with Travellers*.

At one in the morning it was quiet
in the old Simon-community
night shelter on Dublin's Ellis Quay. I
stood at an upstairs window and
watched the river gliding slowly by. A
squad car cruised down the quay,
ignoring the girl standing under the
lamplight.

The building had been condemned
but tonight it was a warm resting place
for over fifty homeless men. I was fairly
nervous, as it was my first time to do
overnight duty and, to make matters

worse, I was on my own due to a shortage of voluntary workers. Earlier one of the men had tried to test my mettle by throwing one of his shoes at me. On the spur of the moment I just threw the shoe back at him. We exchanged a few expletives and then the two of us laughed and he made his way to the bed where he was now sleeping like a baby.

Two beds down Corky was twisting and turning. He was more nervous than me. He was hoping to visit his daughter the following day and his good clothes were hanging at the back of the bed. I sat down beside him and, like Cork people everywhere, we exchanged stories of the home place. We were born within a mile of each other and he had been baptised and made his First Communion in the Lough Church where my parents were married. Food for thought.

John O'Leary had told me earlier that he would give me a hand with the breakfast in the morning. I hoped he would remember. John was from Kerry, a small sized man with a kind, wrinkled face. Like Corky – and myself – he had held onto his accent through all his years amongst the 'Dubs'. How in the name of God do people like the two of them become homeless? A better question, why do we allow it to happen?

The rays of the early sun had a struggle to get through the grubby kitchen windows. This room held many memories for Simon people. Once, as Christmas Eve became Christmas Day, I saw this kitchen packed with homeless men: rough, sweaty, drunk, sober, lonely.

Then Patrick, who lived nearby in a hovel with his two Alsatian dogs, raised his voice and sang two beautiful songs of home. Such a silence among the men. Such beauty and loveliness in their life-scarred faces. When the songs ended there wasn't even that much applause – it was more like a deep sigh which said we cannot afford to let ourselves think like this for too long. And then the hubbub started again.

Anyway, John and myself managed the breakfast no bother.

Big pots of strong, sweet tea. Boiled eggs – about a hundred of them! A steam-filled kitchen. And slices and slices of bread to be buttered.

Then the day workers came in. I thanked John and then it was time for me to go home. I walked down a bit of the quays with Corky and, before we parted, it seemed right to shake hands with each other.

LANGUAGE

OUGHTERARD LEMONS

Moya Cannon

Moya Cannon lives in Galway and is the author of two poetry collections, *Oar* and *The Parchment Boat*. She was the recipient of the Lawrence O'Shaughnessy award 2001.

I am addicted to placenames and to the stories embedded in them. A few years ago I was told by a musician acquaintance of mine that the housing estate on which he had grown up in Oughterard, Co. Galway, bore the improbable name 'The Lemon Fields'. Allegedly, a local landlord, returned from Spain, had once tried to grow lemons there. My informant claimed to have seen the last remaining stunted lemon tree, complete with miniature lemons, growing in a neighbour's garden in the early 1960s.

I loved what I first saw as the

extravagance of the venture – the audacity of trying to grow lemons in Galway rain and wind. I then began to think about the impulse in most of us, particular after a *first* journey abroad, to bring back something of the savour and the colour of the place we have visited.

This is, after all, how language, culture and agriculture have always travelled – by people bringing with them what they love as well as what they need. Silk, spice and amber carved out some of the great trade routes of the middle ages. There is so little, if anything, which is really native to any area. Even the bedrock has usually travelled vast distances. It is hard for us to believe, for instance, how very recently gigues and quadrilles were brought back to this country by some travelling musician or other. They quickly became naturalised as jigs and reels – the exotic becoming apparently indigenous.

If there is truth in the story of 'The Lemon Fields', it is worth considering that lemon trees may have seemed a reasonably sensible import and no more exotic than the potatoes which Raleigh had brought to the south of the country some centuries earlier. Lemons were known to prevent scurvy on long sea voyages, they tasted wonderful and they were extremely decorative. Trial and error are as essential to our survival as our more measured endeavours. I wrote the following poem as a celebration of the quixotic impulse, which is central to our humanity and, indeed, to our survival.

In Paup Joyce's garden in the sixties
in a council estate called 'The Lemon Fields',
they say there was a bush
with small lemons growing on it.

An O'Flaherty of Aughanure Castle
had once shipped the trees from Spain
and had planted his land with them.

Stranger things had rooted,
had almost gone native –
tubers from the Americas some voyager had brought back –
so why not this counterpoint to honey,
like honey, a love child of the sun.

A whiff of spice roads
and we drag dreams home from our journeys –
necessary evidence of other climates,
other ways of growing –

And some dreams do take root in the quotidian,
as surely as fuchsia rampages along a side-road,
and some sustain us totally, then fail us totally

And some hardly take at all
but survive in the tang of a placename,
in a crazy bush tilted by the wind.

THE GRAVITY OF POETRY

Iggy McGovern

Iggy McGovern lives in Dublin, where he lectures in Physics at Trinity College. A Hennessy Award winner, his poetry has appeared in Irish and international journals.

Richard Feynman once remarked that a Martian observer might reasonably conclude the following: the reason the earth spins is the feverish, collective brushing of teeth by earthlings located at the light/dark boundary on the earth's surface. Our Martian might also speculate that the reason the earth goes around the sun is something to do with school summer holidays. Of course, the real reason is gravity.

Gravity is a very serious word. We speak of the gravity of the situation; mention of the school summer holidays registers high on my gravity meter. And gravity is the cause of much anxiety among the physicists. Gravity is the last big puzzle (for the moment at least), the one of the four fundamental forces in the universe that cannot be unified with the others. And yet, when it comes to poetry, gravity, as Myles would say, is your only man.

The proper answer to the question 'What have physics and poetry got in common?' is *rhythm*. The easiest way to demonstrate rhythm is with the simple pendulum: suspend a small weight on a length of cord and set it swinging; the period of swing varies with the length of cord and is, in fact, proportional to the square root of the length; the other parameter needed for this calculation is the acceleration due to gravity. Indeed, one writer has poetically described gravity as 'the pendulum's silent partner'.

The properties of the simple pendulum were first investigated by Galileo, including the suggestion that the pendulum could be used to construct a clock; moreover, his great contributions as an astronomer paved the way for Newton's theory of gravity; however, Galileo's espousal of a sun-centred universe also brought him into conflict with church authorities, leading to the threat of torture and, upon his recanting of his work, a sentence of house arrest. The eventual apology was a long time in coming.

Gravity and politics are never far apart: the race to put humans in space was a feature of the Cold War; the sputnik that crossed the skies of my childhood had more than one political context. Back then, we did not know that in a satellite the dust accumulates on the floor *and* on the ceiling. The net force on dust particles is in the opposite direction on either side of the zero-gravity line; but then the politics of housework was sub-surface in the 1950s.

More relevant portents, perhaps, have come the other way, that is, from space to us. In the same period a sizeable chunk of meteorite fell to earth in County Tyrone. That it crashed through the roof of an RUC Station seems now like a harbinger of three decades of political violence.

PRAYER

Mark Roper

Mark Roper's poetry collections include *The Hen Ark* (which won the 1992 Aldeburgh Prize), *Catching the Light* and *The Home Fire*. He was Editor of *Poetry Ireland* for 1999.

One New Year's Eve, I met up with some friends in a pub. We spent the night there. It was, in retrospect, a strange night. Other people kept coming over to talk to us. It seemed all these other people wanted to do was to pour their hearts out. They would sit down with us and, next thing we knew, they'd be deep into a long confession.

What did their confessions have in common? They had all had terrible Christmases with their families. Rows, tears, recriminations — it seemed a wonder that anyone had survived the so-called festive season. They all swore they were never going to endure another family Christmas again. New Year's Eve became a kind of group therapy session.

I was reminded of the joke about Einstein's Second Law of Relativity: time passes more slowly with your relatives. But it wasn't all that funny. There was a sense of relief, but it wasn't a case of being able to enjoy New Year's Eve and to look forward to another year. It was a case of having survived Christmas. At the same time, families hadn't really been escaped. There was a kind of desperation in the way people were talking, as if they were really talking to themselves. It was as if a tape was playing inside their heads, which they were powerless to stop.

I suppose that we all carry something like that around inside us. Sometimes it's referred to as 'baggage'. Certain things that have happened to us we can never forget and sometimes our whole life gets based around them. At the worst we blame someone else, as if things could somehow have been different. I don't mean in any way to make light of such feelings. In fact, I'm really trying to stress how strong, how deep, how unalterable they can be. Sometimes our minds are like washing machines. The same old stories go round and round. We can do nothing to stop them.

When such feelings are at their worst, they're very hard to bear. But, if we're lucky, there are moments when all the 'baggage' falls away and gets revealed as something that exists only in the mind. In this poem, 'Prayer', I've tried to put those two states of mind together.

How we survive, Lord. Twenty-two homes,
sixteen schools before we were ten.
Those blind uncles touching us up.
Our wounds wide open, our words not heard
until we wept, but were not allowed to.
O the tears uncried, strained against
the eyes, the good conduct medals.

It's no wonder, Lord. Fingers at
the underwear, fists in the stomach,
stories spooled inside us, pleading
to be repeated. Look at us, crawling
from the wrecks of our childhoods,
begging any stranger for a hug.
O what happened. And what happened.

Let us praise, tonight, ourselves.
Our flesh, bones, eyes, hands, hair,
the brightness of our being.
How should our light not shine?
Look at us, Lord, praise us,
real tonight as each other,
as real as can be. Beyond belief
our beauty, our right to be here.

HOME WORDS
FROM ABROAD

Bernard Share

Bernard Share edited *Books Ireland* and
CARA magazine for Aer Lingus. He has
published novels, social history and
linguistics. His most recent title was a
new edition of *Slanguage: A Dictionary of Slang
and Colloquial English in Ireland.*

The obvious sources of our
colloquial speech are Irish,
English and, in the North, Ulster
Scots, but that is by no means the
whole story. Over the centuries words
have crept into the vocabulary from
many other sources, some of them now
virtually unrecognisable as anything
but the familiar vernacular. It is hard to
credit the fact, for example, that the
'hooley', an accepted feature of the
Irish way of doing things, has its
origins in a word describing a Hindu

festival and was possibly brought back, some suggest, by Irish soldiers in the imperial British armies. The same source has been held accountable for 'conjun box', a familiar term in Cork for a small moneybox. A Tamil word, it was possibly imported at some stage in the nineteenth century by returning Munster Fusiliers.

I say 'possibly', because in the matter of word origins it is very difficult to be positive beyond argument, unless you can catch them almost at the point of entry. Thus we can hazard that the Dublin word 'gurrier' is somehow related to the French *guerrier*, a warrior, but we are far from sure how and when it entered our colloquial speech. On the other hand we can be pretty certain that 'to disappear', deriving from the Troubles in the North and meaning to execute and bury in an unknown grave, owes its presence in our language to the *desaparecidos* who suffered a similar fate in Argentina. Similarly the term 'mingi man', a kind of itinerant salesman who catered to the needs of the Irish troops in the Congo in the 1960s, not only entered the language at that time but also was brought by the same troops – or their colleagues – to the Lebanon where there was, and probably still is, a flourishing band of mingi men. An interesting question, of course, is whether the term will survive in popular speech or disappear like a host of once common colloquial terms. Only time will tell.

Language, particularly colloquial language, is a two-way traffic, and in this respect Ireland has been in the export business since our people began to leave our shores to travel the world, whether voluntarily or otherwise. Thus the English of Australia is rich in Irishisms, from the familiar phrase 'Good on you' (compare the Irish *rinne sé a mhaith orm* – literally 'he did good on me'), to the Kathleen Mavourneen, an indeterminate prison sentence, from the ballad which includes the words 'it may be for years and it may be for ever'. Then there are words like 'sheebeen' which turn up in American speech and, in the colloquial Spanish or Cuba, a word that appears in their

ALL IN A
LANGUAGE

Patricia Nolan

Patricia Nolan, a Dubliner educated in
Capetown, lives in Paris where she worked
for *Newsweek*. She now teaches journalism at
the University of Paris II. Her publications
include *Travelling, Encres Nomade, L'Ireland
Intime* and *Striptease* is published in 2005.

Expressions such as *le shopping, le
parking* and *forwarder un email* are
invading the French language. The
French, once resistant to English, have
now embraced globalisation. They are
flocking to English language schools.

Maybe due to this new openness,
the French government has recently
approved the teaching of certain
regional languages in French schools.
The Bretons and the people of the
Languedoc have campaigned for this
right for years. This new law could

eventually include Berber, the language spoken by over one million Berber emigrants from Algeria. Not Arabs, they speak their own language and have a rich and ancient culture. Famous Berber kings, such as Massinisa, once reigned over North Africa from Libya to Morocco. They fought the Romans and the Carthaginians. The Berbers in Algeria are known as the Kabyl. They are wonderful musicians, poets and writers.

Until recently in France, few people spoke English. One could speak freely in public knowing that relatively few understood what was being said whatever the language.

However, some years ago, a younger sister and my overweight English cousin sat opposite two girls in the metro. It's rare that anybody speaks in the metro. The movement of the train rocks everybody into a state of semi-consciousness.

Suddenly, one of the girls said to the other in Irish, '*Tá sí ana rambair.*' My sister glared at the two girls opposite.

They wriggled in embarrassment. One said to the other, '*Tá súil agam ná tuigeann sí.*' My sister simply said, '*Tuigim.*' My cousin never knew she had been the subject of a conversation in Irish.

But to come back to the Kabyl of Algeria. They have been looking for official recognition of their language and culture for decades. In 1998, the Algerian regime imposed Arabic as the official language of the country. Their law did not take into account the cultural diversity of Algeria. The result has been continual social disturbances and deaths among the Kabyl.

In June, Kabylie commemorated the third anniversary of the assassination of their outspoken singer Matoub Lounes. He symbolised his people's struggle for recognition of their culture. We Irish can emulate the Kabyl by putting a greater effort into preserving the Irish language.

Now that we are prosperous, we could invest more in our native language. I am privileged to speak French and English. I can read my poetry in both languages in francophone and anglophone countries. But I miss being able to read in Irish, although I used to be fluent when younger. I had a wonderful teacher to thank for this. Her name is Sister Margaret Mary from Gortnor Abbey in Mayo.

Some time ago, I met her after a gap of many years. I was introduced in my Anglicised name. She said to me, '*Cad is ainm duit?*' I replied, '*Pádraicin Ní Nualláin is ainm dom.*' Immediately, she knew who I was. I wonder now why I never kept my Irish name. When I tell Kabyl friends my Irish name, they can't understand why I'm called Patricia Nolan. They are literally dying to preserve their language. Every language is unique; it connects us to our history, our myths, our own vision of the world. Future generations will thank us for preserving this richness.

Postscript: In 2002 Berber was recognised as an official language alongside Arabic in Algeria.

LETTERS

Mary Coll

Mary Coll, a freelance writer and broadcaster from Limerick, has published a
collection of poetry, *All Things Considered*,
and contributes regularly to programmes
on RTÉ Radio as well as reviewing for
various magazines and journals.

The postman calls to our house
almost every day, and every day I
still pick up the post expecting to find
an actual letter among the ever-
increasing pile of catalogues and bills.
It's not that I'm waiting for some
special letter in particular. It's just that
it's been so long since anyone wrote to
me, personally, other than a financial
institution, that I actually can't remember who my last letter came from or
what it was about.

I have two telephones, each with
some form of answering machine, I

have e-mail and I have a serious weakness for text messaging; this means that on an average day I communicate with a frequency that keeps at least one satellite orbiting the earth. However, I haven't written a letter in so long I'm not sure if I have notepaper and envelopes that match, and what's worse, I'm no longer even certain that matching stationery is in vogue.

Without giving away too much information, I will admit to coming from the *Insert coins now and press button A* era of communication, which was also still the era of the letter writer – it had to be, because very few of those telephones ever worked properly.

I accept that my letters from Irish College did not mark the beginning of a golden age in correspondence, but from around then, to some ill-defined time recently, I was consistently writing to friends and family, and getting replies from all over the world at a level that made at least one half-decent stamp collection possible. I also kept most of these letters, because it was unthinkable to throw personal letters away and dispose of that unique link between two people, when like a photograph it allows the possibility of a brief return to moments that capture the absolute cadence of your life. Moments that seemed ordinary or unremarkable at the time, until the people you shared them with are no longer there to tell you who won the match or what the weather was like or who got a job. Letters that came faithfully to me every week in Ohio full of details I thought were a little unimportant then. Somewhat more exotic letters from Florence, from the first of my friends who really went to live in Europe before travel became incidental. Small, pale-blue wafer-like letters from Africa, as brief and composed as the life they represented, and then the long neatly typed letter describing a funeral on a hillside above the convent hospital for a family who would never visit the grave. Some stand out, most I have forgotten, but they are all there somewhere in boxes, under beds, up in the attic, all the highs and lows along with a few that might even raise an occasional eyebrow.

Perhaps it's sentimental of me, but I suspect I may not be the only one who double-checks the post. I used to recognise handwriting as quickly as I now recognise the numbers that flash up on my phone. I also think, or perhaps just hope, that I had something more to say than the telegram-style sentences I now send in quick response to receipt of same. When I was still writing letters, and letters were still being written to me, I have a feeling we were all able to read far more between the lines.

THE TANGO
PEOPLE

Judith Mok

Judith Mok was born in Holland and is
now based in Dublin. As a classical singer,
she has travelled the world. She has published three books of poetry and two novels.

T*o come back with a branded brow. More
lines, twenty years is nothing.*

He sings with a baritone voice that
has obviously been cultivated by the
wish for another world. One where it
could set itself to the tune of
Schumann's *Dichterliebe*, for example.
This man with the greying hair on the
naked stage in the ugly light shows his
public the face of a tortured man, a
broken poet, the drama of being alive,
the shameless pathos, the tango.

He is sixty years old and we
celebrate his birthday with food, friendship and a lot of champagne. He has a

brother who speaks of nothing but classical music and the temples where he heard the gods perform. His brother does not speak of tango. They had another brother who sang the great composers. But he could not live.

The tango singer has two daughters, an ex-wife and a Belgian duchess for a mistress. She is the real thing; he likes her because her shoes are old, her sweater is torn and her voice is underdeveloped. So he can hear himself better. But here's the torture: he does not know what it is he wants to hear. Could it be that he wants to hear his life in his tango?

The trouble is what does his life sound like?

Happy birthday, Horacio Molina.

She sits back at the table and smiles the dual smile. The one that knows and does not betray. She has lost the love of her life, first to a lover and then to death. She has stepped on stages and juggled with the classical composers all over the world. Her world. She has also conquered the rawer tunes of her country, Argentina, and she has an affair with the tango.

She tells us about this man – with consuming eyes, a strong embrace, a devilish dancer. A Tango King. She sings with a voice that rings from inside the earth. She breathes the words, *To live with the soul embittered by the sweet memories that made me cry long ago.* We listen with love, like friends do.

Then Patty, the pianist, stands up, walks to her Steinway Grand. She plays Schumann. Suddenly the clean whisper of his music makes us still. A still life of humans seated at a round table in Buenos Aires. The friend who is famous because of his blue eye, still blue at sixty. The singer, his brother and the mistress. The female singer caught in her formal smile. The other female singer from another country. That country where one light spot in a painting brightened up half of the world for centuries. A simple thing, a clear melody. Not much else matters any more.

Me muero, I am dying. The streets hear their voices. Do not leave, stay with your friends. They shout at the bottom of the stairs in the airport. Come back! How cruel it is to leave this country. We don't need it sugar-coated in pathos. Unless it is tango.

Do these wonderful souls think that pathos is real, or worse that pathos is poetry? Pathos is pathos.

And poetry just is.

LA MUERTE ON TV (A HAIBUN)

George Swede

George Swede is a poet and has published
30 books and 18 chapbooks. He lives and
works in Toronto, Canada, but each year
spends a couple of months near Guadal-
ajara, Mexico.

My wife and I lean forward as the
TV shows a bullfighting ring in
Mexico City. The camera focuses on a
closed gate showing the number 21 and
the weight 406 kilograms. Loud mari-
achi music sounds and the gate opens.
Out rushes almost 900 pounds of
testosterone-fuelled anger. The crowd
cheers as the bull circles the empty dirt
ring thrusting his sharp horns at
imaginary foes.

> Mariachi horns blare
> the blood lust crowd and the bull
> excited by each other

The two commentators start using unfamiliar words. In an attempt to follow their patter, we search for our Spanish-English dictionary. By the time we find it, a man on horseback, called a *picador*, is on screen. Dressed in black, he wields a long lance or *pica*. The horse's sides are protected by thick padding coloured orange and yellow and its eyes are completely blindfolded by black material. When the curious bull gets close enough, the *picador* pokes his *pica* at the bulging neck muscle in front of the bull's shoulders. Enraged, the bull attacks the horse, which stumbles, but does not go down because the padding absorbs most of the shock. Then two men in blue matador suits run out. Each is carrying two *banderillas*, shafts covered with purple and blue streamers and ending with harpoon-shaped steel points. The men take turns dancing in front of the perplexed bull, eventually sticking all four of their *banderillas* into the bulging neck muscle already stained red from the *pica*. The *banderillas* can only enter the length of the blade and thus stick out of the bull like party decorations.

festive colours
on the killing ground – red also
in the bull's eyes

At last, the matador emerges. He is young with slick black hair and wears a green suit with pink stockings. His movements are macho, engaging as he tosses a black bullfighter's hat over his shoulder toward the expensive seats. The audience cheers and the TV hosts comment favourably. Waving a red cape or *muleta*, the matador struts towards the bleeding bull and gets it to charge. In a balletic move called a *veronica*, he pivots gracefully to avoid the now lumbering beast. The matador does this twice more and once he even turns his back to the confused bull. The crowd and the commentators love this young man.

unlike the bull
the matador knows

a script exists
the arena flags ripple

Having been weakened by damaged neck muscles and loss of
blood, the bull's aggression is less than half what it was before.
Finally, the bull simply stands and stares. This is the moment for
the *estocada* or sword-thrust. The matador goes to edge of the ring
where a man holds out a sheath from which the matador pulls the
sword used for the kill. It is long and curved downward at the tip
in order that it may penetrate deeply.

a smog-shrouded sun
the smiling matador has no shame
in his dark eyes

The matador struts back to the bull, his sword hidden by the
muleta. He stops in front of the bull and raises the sword above
the bull's head and thrusts into *la muerte*, the kill area between the
bull's shoulders. The bull stands shocked, with sides heaving; then
topples over dead.

after the kill
one small cloud of dust
where the tail
is the last to fall

The matador takes a bow. The crowd applauds and the men
in the booth comment favourably on the *estocada*. As horses start
to drag away the dead bull, commercials appear for several
minutes. When the bullring reappears, the gate shows a new
number and weight. My wife and I are transfixed.

STARS

Pat Boran

Pat Boran was born in Portlaoise in 1963 and currently lives in Dublin. A frequent radio broadcaster, he has published four collections of poems, as well as fiction and non-fiction titles.

I've been thinking about the word 'star', you might say considering it. People when they consider put their hands under their chins and look up at the heavens, the kind of pose you see in Roman statues. In fact that's exactly what the word consider means, the 'con' part meaning 'with' and 'sider' coming from *sidus* meaning 'star'. Musing on the heavens. It's the way words often tell a physical history like that which makes them so addictive.

It's 1993 and I'm in Enniskillen, Co. Fermanagh, for a month as writer-in-residence. The room I'm in in the local library fills up with twenty or so schoolboys and -girls, aged about twelve or thirteen. Some Protestant, others Catholic. The ones in grey are the Protestants – or is it the Catholics? Either way, it's important to know they're different.

'Say the word "star"', I say to the nearest girl. 'Stor,' she says, somewhat puzzled. Then I have them all say it. 'Stor', 'sthor', 'store', 'sthair', until there is a night sky hovering above us, the library we're sitting in has vanished for the moment and we can be ourselves again, children who like to play with words beneath the sky.

The dictionary says the word 'pupil' comes from the Latin *pupila*, meaning little doll.

'The wolf,' I say, 'represents the dark, the hidden side of the pigs.'

We've been discussing my favourite fairytale, my favourite story, actually, the *Three Little Pigs*. There's something incredibly satisfying about hearing it yet again. We've been talking about how, when the wolf and the last little pig finally meet, the pig finds a tiny version of himself in the wolf's eye and the wolf finds himself hiding in the pig's! As if on cue, two soldiers in camouflage pass by the window. We are in the pupils of their eyes, as they are in the pupils of ours.

There's a picture of a ship run aground stuck up on the felt board at the front of the room. It's an impressive sight: the enormity of this man-made vessel against a line of men who look like little more than insects trying, if you can believe your eyes, to drag it over the land.

My students have to write about this ship, this beach, these tiny ant-like people. They have to write and read out what they write to the rest of group, often doing so in the voices of strangers.

'My name is Chang,' one says (it's not), 'and I am Chinese and I come here every day to try to pull this ship.'

'And my name is Stavinski,' another says, and gives another explanation.

And there are Irish men and women, and English men and

women, and Martian invaders caught without reserve fuel, their great hulk of a ship stuck fast in the surface of an alien planet, and as many other stories as we have time for.

But the Catholics, Protestants, Chinese and Martians are pulling the same ropes now – word ropes – not only as if they had to shift this rusting hulk we have to deal with, but also as if their common efforts might draw out more stars in the sky.

EDWARD THOMAS
AND THE OWL

Ciaran O'Driscoll

Ciaran O'Driscoll lives in Limerick. He
has published five poetry collections, most
recently *Moving On, Still There — New and
Selected Poems*. He has also published a
memoir *A Runner Amongst Fallen Leaves* and
was the first recipient of the Patrick and
Katherine Kavanagh Fellowship in Poetry.

In Umbria, Italy, one starry night last
October, I stood on the edge of the
oak woods listening to the cry of an
owl. It was the first time I realised the
accuracy of Edward Thomas's poem,
which described the cry as 'shaken out'.
And shaken out it was, this owl's cry. It
had a quiver in it. And the quiver,
together with the pitch of the note,
gave it an extraterrestrial dimension;
something to put the hair standing on
the back of the head.

Downhill I came, hungry and yet not starved;
Cold, yet had heat within me that was proof
Against the North wind; tired, yet so that rest
Had seemed the sweetest thing under a roof.

Then at the inn I had food, fire and rest,
Knowing how hungry, cold and tired was I.
All of the night was quite barred out except
An owl's cry, a most melancholy cry.

Shaken out long and clear upon the hill,
No merry note, nor cause of merriment,
But one telling me plain what I escaped
And others could not, that night, as in I went.

The geese in the compound are nervous tonight. Every now
and then there is a clatter of honking and a shuffling as they shift
from one part of their enclosure to another. Perhaps they are
simply continuing into darkness their silly daylight game of who's
in authority. But the cry of this owl is enough to make any goose
nervous, enough to raise goose pimples.

I first heard Edward Thomas's poem in the early 1960s, on a
Caedmon record; LP or EP, I forget, but it was unforgettably
recited by another Thomas – Dylan. Almost forty years later, in
the autumn of the year 2000, listening to an Umbrian owl, I get
the same shiver up the spine as I did when I first heard the poem.
And the poem has come back into my head in its entirety, as if
the cry had unlocked memory. We are living in Artane, Dublin.
We have a well-battered gramophone, on which my teenage
sister wants to play Helen Shapiro and I want to play Dylan
Thomas ... Time passes, tick-tock, tick-tock; it's the opening of
an episode of *The Twilight Zone*.

Down the road in Orvieto, Signorelli's frescoes *The Four Last
Things* are undergoing extensive refurbishment. Here in the heart

of the countryside, an owl's cry almost forces me to consider them: Death, Judgement, Hell and Heaven. But for one still hale and hearty, these are all purely aesthetic phenomena: a tragedy, a ghost story, Signorelli's frescoes, an owl's cry. They're good for a thrill. Have we lost the 'connectedness' that stood the goose pimples out on earlier generations and societies, bringing people into the presence of their own death?

And salted was my food, and my repose,
Salted and sobered, too, by the bird's voice,
Speaking for all who lay under the stars,
Soldiers and poor, unable to rejoice.

Edward Thomas's poem is almost a premonition of impending death. He was killed in action during the First World War. Maybe with hindsight we can now understand the poem for what it really is: the poet confronting his fate in advance, his fate announced by the owl's cry. *Shaken out long and clear upon the hill.*

There is no conventional, comfortable 'to-whit, to-who'. It makes me wonder how Shakespeare ever said that the owl sang 'a merry note'. Perhaps he was listening to a different owl.

LUNAR LANDING

Vincent Woods

Vincent Woods was born in Co. Leitrim in 1960. Playwright, poet and former radio journalist, his work for theatre includes *At The Black Pig's Dyke* and his poetry *Lives and Miracles*. He is a member of Aosdána.

Poems can have a strange genesis. A few years ago I was driving from Sligo to Leitrim at night and as I turned a bend in the road the moon was huge on Lough Gill – in it, almost. For a moment I felt this pull, this surge to drive the car into the moon in the water – to land, splash on the moon – drown in it.

I resisted, but a poem came by a short time after – and this is the thing, poems *do* come by. We're not sure where they come from, we can dream them, almost remember them, conjure them – but sometimes the poem seems to conjure itself through us. And there's the rub — how do we rationally explain inspiration, the times when words flow through us, when the artist's pencil or brush or pen moves with speed and certainty out and beyond what is planned or anticipated? It's one of the joyful mysteries of life and I do not believe science will ever explain it. Not fully. Never.

Like the feelings we get sometimes in a particular place — feelings of pain or suffering; of well-being or great love — the *féar gorta*, hungry grass of life-force thwarted or exalted.

So from the moon in a lake on a winter's night comes a narrative, and a character or two, and a story that is a true lie — something that never happened, yet must have happened; that may never happen, yet occurs each time this poem is read. Each time the person who never existed, Francie McPadden, sits into his car and the barman looks up at the moon and remembers:

Lunar Landing

You all think, the barman said,
You all think that Neil Armstrong
Was the first man on the moon.
Well, you're wrong —
Because he wasn't.
You see Francie McPadden
Was going home this night
And a good fourteen or fifteen
Pints in his belly.

There was a full moon
(It was July)
And there's a hoor of a bend
In the road out there be the cross.

Francie took it in top
And it seems he was blinded
By the moonlight
And the old Cortina went splash
Into the lake –
Right into the moon
In the water.

So you could say Francie landed
Well ahead of Armstrong.

Only he didn't come back.

I LOVE ME

Peter van de Kamp

Peter van de Kamp (1956) lives in Bally-roe, Co. Kerry, with his wife Caroline and his dog Mickey.

A couple of years ago I invented a party game, which requires nothing but a warped sense of humour and a memory for lyrics. It's given me and others hours of harmless fun, and I want to share it with you. All you do is change the second person pronoun in a song to the first. The results are unforgettable. Thus I can be heard singing under the shower:

> The more I see me, the more I love me.
> Can I imagine as time goes by
> You know the only one for me can only be me ...

or what about:

> Why do birds suddenly appear
> Every time I am near; just like me
> They want to be close to me.

or the perennial, and somewhat less subtle

> I love me, yeah, yeah, yeah.

We were playing this game some years ago on the last night of KISS, our Kerry International Summer School of Living Irish Authors. Contributions were flowing round the room more abundantly than porter, when in one of those lulls of thought a dear lady-friend, one of the most correct people I've ever met, came up with the gem of the night – its fun being heightened by its being so out of character. The lady's eyes lit up, as she set in:

> I'll be coming round the mountain when I come

She continued, like Lady Godiva, and capped it all with an ecstatic finale, 'shouting hallelujah'.

Of course, I have a reason for sharing this game with you, other than sheer ribaldry. Love may have been introduced in our Western culture in the middle ages by the troubadours, as C. S. Lewis informs us. And our time-honoured forefathers may have considered it a disease, the proverbial 'toothache'. But it has nestled itself securely, and thankfully, into our *raison d'être*. However, and this is my point, it seems to have undergone a change of late, what with its over-commercialisation in pop culture. The air is thick with songs about love, but the heart has grown thinner in all this exultation. In the old days we were taught, quite rightly of course, to love our neighbours; nowadays that noble maxim seems to have been replaced by the dictum that we must love ourselves, and that we must love ourselves before we can love anybody else. My answer to that facile piece of self-help psychology is: take one lyric, change the 'you' into 'I', and the validity of the advice is shown up for what it's worth.

I'm afraid Oscar Wilde got it wrong: self-love is not the beginning of a life-long romance.

KINDERGARTEN

Thomas F. Walsh

Thomas F. Walsh, compiler of the *Favourite Poems We Learned in School* series, was born in Headford, Co. Galway. He has written a number of short stories and a memoir called *Once in a Green Summer*. Formerly a primary-school headmaster in Dublin, he is now a writer and broadcaster.

One of my favourite words of all time is the word 'kindergarten'. It conjures up such a wondrous picture of that first learning space we give our children: 'kindergarten', German for 'the children's garden'. And recently, when I came across a book called *All I Really Need to Know I Learned in Kindergarten*, I just had to buy it. A man called Robert Fulghum wrote it and it's a book about life, about simple truth and everyday living. These are the things I learned in kindergarten, Fulghum says:

Share everything.
Play fair.
Don't hit people.
Put things back where you found them.
Clean up your own mess.
Don't take things that aren't yours.
Say you're sorry when you hurt somebody.
Wash your hands before you eat.

Everything you need to know is in there somewhere, Fulghum reminds us, The Golden Rule and love and basic sanitation. Ecology and politics and equality and sane living. And you can't argue with his thesis. Just think how much better off the world would be if we lived by those rules. If we all shared everything and played fair. If we all, including governments, had a basic policy to always put things back where we found them and cleaned up our own mess.

I often wonder at what precise stage children stop doing as we say and start imitating what we do. And I think that it is only in the world of childhood that the secret of the world lies. To a child a promise is an empty thing; their joy is in the now.

There was once a time when people could live happily by the wisdom of the child. The Blasket Islanders were the rearguard of such a race, unsullied by sophistication. *An t-Oileánach*, Tomás Ó Criomhthain's account of the last inhabitants, contains a quotation that has remained with me always. He tells of the arduous journey to the mainland to sell the cattle and how, after the fair, they contemplated going home to the hardship and the hard work of the island. No, said an older man in the company, they would wait another day and rest and enjoy a drink while they could. '*Lá d'ár saol é,*' he said. 'It's a day in our life.' A wise old poet said the same thing in another language. '*Carpe Diem,*' he said. 'Seize the day.' Live in the now.

They say that all true artists create from that inner stillness of the present moment. Wordsworth was such a one:

My heart leaps up when I behold
A rainbow in the sky:
So was it when my life began;
So be it when I shall grow old,
Or let me die!
The child is father of the man.

And when the path of life is fading near the end, we know that there is often drawn around us a sheltering veil of simplicity, a 'second childhood' we sometimes call it. We leave the wilderness and come back into the children's garden.

All we ever need to know we learned in kindergarten.

The Past

Silence in Wicklow

Ellen O'Toole

Ellen O'Toole lives in Wicklow, has three cows, fights briars and cultivates bumble-bees. She writes when it is raining.

Whenever I'm in Wicklow, travelling the road from Aughrim to Greenane on my way to Glenmalure I let down the window of the car just before I reach Greenane and broadcast Radio na Gaeltachta — quietly. It is, at one level, a ridiculous gesture. At another level it is all someone like myself can do to send a message back in time, to tell the ghosts that there are still people around who speak the same language, who care.

On the right-hand side of this

road, as you go towards Greenane, there is the museum of farm implements, well signposted. There are signs for it from as far away as Calary Bog. And it is well worth a visit.

On the left, on private land, there is a ring fort, once the *dún* of the O'Byrne Clann. Fiach Mac Hugh O'Byrne was the 'firebrand of the Wicklow hills', who held out for so long against the forces of Queen Elizabeth and who won the battle of Glenmalure in 1580 – one of the very few battles that the Irish actually won. There is no sign to indicate the presence of this *dún*, nothing to preserve or protect it. Lucky for us that the present owner has a sense of history and can recite the ballad of Fiach McHugh that she learned at school some seventy years ago.

It was in this *dún* that the *Leabhar Branach* was compiled. Because the O'Byrnes were among the few Irish Chieftains who could still afford patronage in the sixteenth century, everybody who was anybody in the *Poetry Ireland* of the time turned up on the doorstep in Baile na Corra.

Tadhg Dall Ó hUigínn came here and left a poem behind him – by his own account he found it a rather wild place and only came to let a political situation he had created at home quieten down a little. Feargal Óg Mac an Bhaird came to the *dún*. Feargal Óg might be considered the first modern Irish poet, since he braved bardic convention and composed poetry in the open air – actually on horseback! – his critics claimed.

Poets would have been rewarded with Spanish wine, gold, silk, perhaps a horse – the proceeds of a dawn raid on Arklow or Wicklow or even a longer strike as far away from Glenmalure as Tallaght or Crumlin.

The *Leabhar Branach* has been called a 'jewel of late Bardic poetry'. In it there are conventional court poems, dedicated to the chieftains of the O'Byrne Clan over several generations. There are poems in it that throw an interesting light on the women of the clann. Most famous of these was Fiach Mac Hugh's second wife, Róis Ní Thuathail. Róis was a 'political activist'. She was confined, at least twice, in Dublin Castle, where she was condemned to be burnt as a witch. She escaped that fate and lived a long life, continuing to the end to conspire against the English, as the State Papers complain rather peevishly. There are a number of harrowing poems in the *Leabhair Branach*, composed when Fiach Mac Hugh was finally defeated, beheaded, quartered and exposed on a rail outside Dublin Castle. The best-known one is by Aonghas Ó Dálaigh:

A cholann do-chím gan cheann,
sibh d'fhaicsin do shearg mo bhríogh.

How many Irish people know anything at all about the *Leabhar Branach*, about the *dún* where it was compiled, about Feilim's castle on the hill above, now swallowed in forestry?

It is a silence that grieves me. So just after passing the farm museum I open the left-hand window and, if it is a Sunday afternoon, let Seán Bán Breathnach give the ghosts the latest sports news — as Gaeilge.

TOM SWIFT AND THE AMAZING AI MAN

Brian Leyden

Brian Leyden was born in Arigna, Co. Roscommon. His books include the short-story collection *Departures*, the novel *Death & Plenty* and his best-selling memoir *The Home Place*.

I had my head stuck in a book of science fiction called *Tom Swift and His Amazing 3-D Telejector* when my father told me to call the AI. The decision to try Artificial Insemination, instead of walking our cow to the nearest bull, was my father's idea to improve the quality of an ageing herd. Holding the exact amount of coins for the call hard in my fist I raced swiftly to the nearest telephone.

When I reached the shop at the foot of the mountain I blurted to the owner, 'Hello Mrs Gillhooley, we have a cow on the rambles.'

She escorted me to the public phone and wound the handle on the side to rouse the post office switchboard. The switchboard called the main exchange. From there the operator called the AI's local dispatch office. Knowing if I got it wrong I hadn't the price of another call, I gingerly fed my coins into three different slots and pressed button A on the moneybox. The right order of coins went down. I was through to the AI.

'When did you notice her?' they asked.

'This morning,' I said.

'Is it her first time?'

It had never occurred to me to ask was our cow a virgin. I wasn't even sure I was supposed to know what the word meant.

'I think so,' I stammered. Realising only after I said it they wanted to know if the AI had been called out before to inseminate the same cow. There was no charge for a repeat call, but it was a black mark against the AI to have too many repeat calls resulting in late spring calving.

'Watch the Skies' – the American B movies urged citizens to beware of alien spacecraft arriving to conquer our world. I kept an equally keen lookout until a car pulled up in our farmyard and I shouted: 'The AI man is landed.'

Ignoring the warning to 'keep out from under the man's feet', I watched a slim tube being extracted from a canister, wafting a dry-ice haze like the liquid oxygen and nitrogen teeming from the sides of a Saturn V rocket on the launch pad at Cape Canaveral.

With a clear plastic glove reaching up his arm, the AI man took the tube to our cow in the barn. Afterwards we left out a bar of carbolic soap, a hard towel and a bucket of lukewarm water for him to scrub up. Apart from this simple courtesy, a docket and the discarded launch tube were the only trace of his visit.

But nine months later we had a totally new breed of animal on the farm: our first Charolais-cross calf. The future had arrived, not in the form of 3-D telejectors or the flying saucer I longed to find secretly landed in our far meadow, but in the shape of an AI man up to his elbows in animal health and worried about repeat calls.

Smoking

Frank Marshall

Frank Marshall lives in Kilkenny. His
drama, prose and poetry have been broadcast by RTÉ lyric fm and Radio Kilkenny.
He contributes regularly to the Dominican
publication *Spirituality*.

When my filing cabinet refused to
open because of the quantity
of stuff I had jammed into it over the
years, it was clear it was time to face
the fact that I was a hoarder. The
decision was a long time coming, but
eventually I brought some humour to
it and was actually smiling at my
weakness when I discovered a
voluminous file marked 'Donnelly
Visas'. This resurrected some very
unsettling memories.

In the late eighties and early
nineties, thousands of Irish people
emigrated to the USA under a quota

system introduced after much lobbying by a few US Congressmen. There is little doubt that the famous Green Cards opened up unlimited possibilities for many who would otherwise have been confined to the humiliation of the dole queue.

The outbreak of the Gulf War in 1991 raised some serious issues for the holders of the Green Cards, when it was revealed that there was a possibility of being drafted into the US forces. What had seemed a harmless paragraph now loomed as a stark reality. It is unclear just how many were actually aware that they could end up in the Middle East opposing the forces of Saddam Hussein.

My two sons were working happily in New Jersey when the awful truth dawned. The phone lines were buzzing nightly across the Atlantic for a few weeks. I will never forget the night of 21 January when I heard a newscaster announce that Mr Bush had authorised the calling up of 20,000 extra into the armed forces. I was unable to sleep that night and at 4 a.m. I sat downstairs, smoking my pipe, wondering what was going to develop. It happened that I had just enlisted in a poetry group, so I tried to commit my troubled thoughts to a blank page. Eventually this emerged as part of the first poem I published.

Two Donnelly Visas equals two sons
Equals two US Marines
Masters' Degrees and Leaving Certs
Are excellent weapons, designed to kill.

The crisis passed. My sons were not drafted and went on to become naturalised US citizens. Over the following decade I travelled over to visit them, almost every year. Once I had cleared US Immigration at Shannon, I treated myself to a glass of Irish whiskey to set me afloat across the Atlantic. It always seemed the right thing to do.

The first year that Kevin was installed in his own home I had negotiated a smoking room for my odoriferous pipe. The following year, when I assumed the same arrangement would apply, he told me that as his wife, Deirdre, was pregnant, it would not be possible for me to smoke in the house. His manner was very apologetic and he seemed quite embarrassed. I can still remember his expression and the concern it revealed. This was a moment of some significance. The boy had become a man and the father had become, well, not an errant child, but he was taking the directions.

Kevin came outdoors with me. It was a warm, balmy September evening in Boston and it turned into a pleasant interlude in the fading light, once the initial embarrassment had softened. Our relationship had always been special but had undergone a perceptible transformation once he was married. 'For this reason a man shall leave his Father and Mother and cling to his wife.'

On subsequent visits I settled happily on a bench in the garden and smoked quite contently. There was an apartment block visible from my position and my imagination was given plenty of scope as the tenants moved about. There was even a group on the top storey who had clearly gathered to smoke.

There is a change of location now. Kevin and Deirdre and three lovely grandchildren have relocated to Greystones. Boston is no longer on the map and smoking is less attractive outdoors in this climate. I stick with my addiction. However there has been one unexpected development in that my four-year-old granddaughter, Heather, is not too fussed by my pipe. The refrain of 'No smoking in the house, Granddad' is often heard in an imperious voice, followed by her screeching, mocking laughter. Even on the phone she scolds me, but the laugh raises my heart like nothing has ever done before.

A non-smoker would never have heard that beautiful, lifting, mocking sound of joy.

RING OUT THE OLD, RING IN THE NEW

Gabriel Fitzmaurice

Gabriel Fitzmaurice was born 1952 in the village of Moyvane, Co. Kerry, where he still lives, teaching in the local National School. He is the author of over thirty books, including collections of poetry in English and Irish and verses for children.

Customs are important, not in as much as they preserve the past, but in that they keep it alive. I am no fanatical conservationist – the past holds no preservation order over me. But I want to let the past live in me. We cannot live in the past, but the past can live in us. That is why I like to see old customs passed on.

So, we ring out the old year. Or, at least, we used to. I remember ringing out the old year about 1970 in

Moyvane. I would have been about eighteen years old and in Leaving Certificate year in secondary school. I was determined to go out on the street to ring out the old, ring in the new. I could persuade nobody to join me. All my friends were going to dances in the neighbouring towns. They abandoned me to my scheme. In those years the pubs closed before midnight. The drinkers dispersed. I had almost given up when a friend of mine, a university student, emerged from some corner of the village. He had a mouth organ. So had I. We stood in the centre of the deserted village and sucked music from our humble instruments. Tennyson was on my Leaving Cert. course, so I stood at Brosnan's Corner and recited at the top of my voice:

Ring out, wild bells, to the wild sky,
The flying cloud, the frosty night:
The year is dying in the night;
Ring out, wild bells, and let him die.

Ring out the old, ring in the new,
Ring, happy bells, across the snow;
The year is going, let him go …

Sometime about one o'clock we called it a night. The following morning as I strolled out, the villagers (at least those who couldn't sleep because of our midnight ceremony) were annoyed. Was the custom dead?

Twenty-something years later Maurice Heffernan, then Chairman of the local Wrenboy group, and I decided to revive the custom. He could let us have the Wrenboys' torches (metal containers mounted on wooden polls in which were held blazing sods of turf soaked in diesel); he could organise musicians. Could I organise the crowd? First things first – musicians and torchbearers were organised. Gathering a crowd was a different matter. When I asked some teenagers if they'd like to ring out the old year, they looked puzzled and asked me what it was. Yes! It had come to that.

It was midnight. The musicians assembled – banjo, tin whistle, accordion, mandolin and bodhrán. The torchbearers lit their torches and raised them up into the night. Carrying our own light, we marched through the village. Through the open doors of midnight, drinkers spilled from pubs. We marched up and down the village and halted at the cross where we played and danced, wished each other a happy New Year and sang 'Auld Lang Syne' before we dispersed. In the following years the practice declined. Bad weather, absent musicians and lack of enthusiasm contributed.

But I, or anyone who saw it, will never forget that first night when the village marched through the doors of midnight into a new year: singing, dancing, making music, carrying its own light, the seed of which might fire a youngster's imagination in years to come to revive the past again.

FATHERHOOD

Dermot Bolger

Dermot Bolger is a poet, playwright and novelist. His ninth novel, *The Family on Paradise Pier*, is published in 2005. He edited the *Picador Book of Contemporary Irish Fiction* and the collaborative novels *Finbar's Hotel* and *Ladies Night at Finbar's Hotel*. A new volume of poems, *The Chosen Moment*, appeared in 2004.

Let me tell you a story told to me by a novelist friend. It occurs in the remote northern part of his native Sweden several years ago. Winter, a desolate snow-bound road, sub-zero temperatures and a car that breaks down a hundred miles from the city he is returning to with his family.

Whatever brief light exists is fading as he trudges to the nearest village with his wife and two small children. Naturally there isn't a garage. Real men fix their own cars up here, he is told. There isn't a bus or a hotel either. Eventually he is told that if he can find a certain barn in the woods somebody there might take pity on him.

When he finds it he's not so sure. It's where the local hard men hang out, souping up their jeeps, spending the long winter tinkering with pistons and spark plugs. They observe him in silence as he tells his story, enjoying his discomfort. Shaved heads, arms thick as the walls of Limerick jail, eyes like hard sweets from Bray that would break your teeth. The rural, urban animosity is the same the world over. Nothing much happens up there in winter, but, by God, the night the city slicker got stranded, unable to fix his own bloody car, will be a story to savour on many evenings to come. He is on his own, they let him know in no uncertain terms. He drove the car, he can fix it.

He opens the barn door to leave, muttering something about getting back to his children. Children? What children? Why the hell didn't he mention children before? The hard men suddenly surround him. What age is his little girl? Is she frightened, cold? One man is producing a photo from his wallet of his daughter who is the same age. Other men are reaching for their coats, a hubbub of male voices laughing companionably as they jostle him out the door, grabbing their tools, demanding directions to the car.

He walks among them, looking at their open faces. They have ceased to be men, he realises, suddenly they have all become fathers.

Ever since being told of that incident, I think of it a lot when I am with other men. Maybe Masonic lodges are the same with their secret codes and handshakes, but fatherhood is a strange invisible bond, linking the most unlikely of people.

People look back at society thirty and forty years ago and say that it was a man's world. On almost every practical level they are absolutely right, most especially when the most obvious symbol of fatherhood today, all too often, is the shabby bed-sit a few miles from the spacious family home. Forty years ago men certainly held all the cards, with property rights, women forced to leave many jobs when they married, biased inheritance laws and the unwritten law that women were meant to suffer in silence behind closed doors while authority turned a blind eye.

The marvellous poet Michael Hartnett once summed up a chilling portrait of Christmas Eve at that time as being a night when 'in pubs the men filled up with porter and in the homes the women filled up with apprehension'.

And yet – for all that – they were prisoners too, trapped within the hard circle of their own maleness. Perpetually in fear of the public ridicule summed up by The Citizen in *Ulysses*, who, upon hearing that Bloom was once seen buying baby food for his son that died, snorts and remarks scornfully, 'Call that a man?'

Even in literature Irish fathers seem trapped in the same boat. The silent, sour, tyrannical head of the family runs through Irish fiction right up through John McGahern and Shane Connaughton and even into very recent novels by the likes of Kate O'Riordan and Colm O'Gaora. What makes Roddy Doyle's *The Snapper* such a radical book isn't just having an unmarried mother as the heroine, but the fact that the book's hero is her own father, a bumbling, well-meaning, slightly bewildered figure, who doesn't chastise but learns to celebrate and bears his grandchild home in triumph.

Irish writers could well argue that, up to now, there were too few of Roddy Doyle's Mrs Rabbitts in real life and too many of John McGahern's Michael Morans.

Maybe they were right, but on summer evenings in playgrounds or wet mornings in adventure centres I see other fathers now. Clambering down narrow slides after their laughing children, pushing prams proudly, rocking teething infants on their knees, immersed totally in the second glimpse at wonder that is given to them by being fully a part of their children's childhood.

Sometimes our eyes meet for a second and I think we are thinking the same thing. Not that it was a man's world for our fathers and grandfathers, but just how much of this short-lived (and never to be repeated) wonder did they miss out on, in that cage of manhood which society trapped them into.

My own father was at sea for all my childhood. His homecomings were joyous events. But too often the coming home of a father was something for children to be threatened with. They were the breadwinners, the rule enforcers, the hardmen out in their barn in the woods waiting for one chance to let the mask slip and produce the photographs of their children, which they carried close to their breasts.

WOLVES

G.V. Whelan

G.V. Whelan is an Irish-Canadian writer
and critic. She has a BA in Celtic Studies
and Philosophy, and an MA in Mediaeval
Irish History. She writes for adults and
young adults under the pen-name OR
Melling. Her books have been translated
into Japanese, Chinese, Russian, Slovenian
and Czech. She lives at present in her
hometown of Bray, Co. Wicklow, with her
daughter, Findabhair.

I stand nervously before the classroom
of Native kids and adults on the
Hay River Reserve in the Northwest
Territories of Canada's subarctic. As a
visiting author I have been invited here,
but I know too much history not to
feel ashamed. Though the Irish
suffered the same trail of tears
inflicted upon the first peoples of
North America, we were not innocent
bystanders when their race fell. We

were one of the European hordes who overran this land, killing and stealing and laying so much to waste. Later still, in the 1950s and 1960s, when an entire generation of Native children were forcibly removed from their families and put into institutions across Canada, Irish clergy were prominent in that system.

The 'residential schools' were ostensibly set up to teach Native children the English language and culture, to help them assimilate into modern society. Torn from their homes and villages, forbidden to use their own languages, clothing, songs or stories, they were beaten and brutalised, physically and sexually assaulted. The Christian churches, both Catholic and Protestant, and the Canadian government who established the system have only begun to pay out compensation, while a lost generation still struggles to recover.

The children of that generation sit before me now. In some I can see the scars of Foetal Alcohol Syndrome and a certain wariness. The older ones in the back are from the adult education class. There is no overt hostility, but the question hangs in the air — who is this white woman standing here and what could she possibly say that would be of any interest to us?

'My last name is Whelan,' I tell them. 'That's the English version of my family name, which is Faolan. In ancient days the Irish believed they were descended from animals, and the oldest families in Ireland still bear the names of their origins. *Faol* is the old Irish word for wolf. Every O'Faolan belongs to the wolf.'

There are nods of recognition. Nothing I have said is strange to them. All Native peoples have animal ancestors, spirit guides or totems. There's the faint promise of kinship in the room, but it's been a long time since my race was connected to that part of their past.

'Are there wolves in Ireland?' one of the kids asks me.

Though the wolf competes with Native hunters, he is held in high regard, and some First Nations, such as the Dene Chipewyan, consider him in the same category as the dog — a brother to humans.

'The modern Irish word for wolf is *mac tíre* – son of the land,' I explain. 'But there are no wolves in Ireland. They were considered a threat to farming, and a bounty was put on their heads. The last Irish wolf was killed at Wolf Hill near Belfast in the late 1700s.'

There were questions, then, about the Irish words I had used. 'English is not your ancestral tongue?'

'No,' I answer, 'but most of my people do not speak their own language. We were a conquered race. There are things we have yet to fully recover.'

More nods of recognition. Again there is a familiarity to what I have said, and I can feel the warmth, the welcome now. It's like the song Susan Aglukark sings, the Inuit pop singer they call the Arctic Rose: *O siem we are all family. O siem we're all the same.*

By the end of my visit I'm reluctant to leave. We have so much to talk about. I am invited to go wolf-calling that night. There's a place on the reserve, near a cliff, where chicken carcasses are dumped and the wolves gather to eat. The wild wolves know the difference between human and wolf howls, but they'll answer anyway just for fun.

I really wanted to go, but my schedule didn't allow it. I was flying out that afternoon for Fort Simpson, further west.

'I'll be back one day,' I swore, 'or my name's not Faolan.'

DREAM-TIME ON THE CAPE SHORE

Michael Coady

Michael Coady is a member of Aosdána and has been the recipient of literary awards at home and abroad. His books include *All Souls* and *One Another*, each integrating poetry, prose and photographs.

Our ancestors called Newfoundland 'Talamh an Éisc', the fishing ground. Around the island of Newfoundland was the proverbially rich cod fishery, exploited over centuries by the Basques, the Portuguese, the French and the English. Here was one of the world's richest sources of protein in the form of a seemingly unlimited supply of fish that could be harvested, preserved by drying and salting and traded in Europe.

By the eighteenth century the Irish

of the lower valleys of the sister rivers Suir, Nore and Barrow had joined the transatlantic trade in an intimately localised migration. The Déise-based poet Donncha Rua MacConmara is said to have journeyed to Talamh an Éisc in 1758 and wrote poems referring to it. Thousands sailed annually out of Waterford, first as seasonal migrant labourers in the fishery and then as settlers in the remote and rocky coves of Newfoundland. The land was poor, but the sea rich. Life was a harsh struggle with elemental things.

In time those pre-Famine Irish communities of Talamh an Éisc were forgotten in homeland memory, their story overshadowed and obscured by the later great exodus to the United States. But, in the physical isolation of Newfoundland fishing settlements, deep pockets of Irishness remained remarkably intact for generations and still leave their strong imprint on the island, which voted to become a province of Canada in 1949.

Mass communication and travel have now brought rapid change everywhere, but when I travelled on the Cape Shore of the Avalon Peninsula in Newfoundland ten years ago, I still heard astonishing echoes of the speech of Waterford and South Tipperary, Kilkenny and Wexford from people generations removed from Ireland.

At Dunville Sunset Home, listening to the old-timers, I could have been on the Irish, rather than the north-American, side of the ocean. 'Some racket they makes, talkin' in their dreams every night,' said Kitty Power, pouring me tea. 'I doubts some o' them crathurs knows the differ' between the livin' and the dead.'

And that's the dream-state of my poem.

After dark when lights are dim
and eyelids down
the sleeping racket rises

among old-timers out of
Branch, Point Lance,
St Brides and Angels Cove.

They dream of whales and winters
of children, rum and storms,
priests and rowing dories

of drownings and of meadows,
dances and salt fish,
moose and muzzleloaders.

The dead rise up behind
closed eyes and stir
in toothless jaws.

Lost in his second sleep, Bill
Foley and his father navigate
in fog without a compass

Phil Tobin, who's a hundred,
splits fish with old Careen
who's buried in The Barrens

and Bridget Brennock plays
with her dead sister by
the brook in Gleann an Cheo

named by the first Breachnach
who settled there from Waterford
forgotten lives ago.

THE COMET

Rowan Hand

Rowan Hand is a Father, Grandfather, Boatman, Swimmer, Cook, Journalist, Writer, Broadcaster, Fledgling Buddhist, Friend, Optimistic Agnostic, Star Gazer, 'Politician' and Lucky, Fatter, Older, Slower, Dreamer, Listener, Talker, Lover of life and all who live it.

It had been the way it used to be and a ship with tall masts and much canvas, accompanied by a flotilla of smaller Tall Ships, was back in Newry. My boat, not a ship, not a yacht, but a Norwegian Folkboat of mahogany on oak, lay to her ropes and, below, in the lamplight, men of the sea talked of other times. The occasion emboldened and allowed the taking of poetic liberties:

I will have my boat in a still place
Away from the raging sea
And men who were boys when I was a boy
Will sit and talk with me.

This St Patrick's Day was one of the most memorable ever in the town of Newry. The ships were coming back into the ancient and wonderful waterway that is the Newry Ship Canal, the Victoria Lock allowing passage in from the sea. It was the Newry tradition, handed down from father to son, from family to family.

This great event of nauticalia commemorated the leaving of Newry in other times of exiles fleeing the Famine of different ships, 'Coffin Ships', outward bound to a new world of hope. Many would make it and survive, others wouldn't and, for this occasion, the descendants of those who made a new life were back in Newry.

Hale Bobb wasn't known about at the time of the Famine. It would have been wending its icy way on a forty billion mile orbit of the universe and now, like the rest of us, it was back, low in the north-eastern sky, trailing luminosity and taking its place in the symphony of celebration that we were all part of.

The man at the oil lamp by the cabin door got up. Peadar is a barrel-chested, tough gentleman of the sea; had he been an early follower of the Christian God he, most assuredly, would have been a Peter.

The turf was burning well in the grate down below. We sat hunched in the cramped cabin space like creatures packed and voyaging through the unknown.

Peadar shook himself and went outside into the darkness to greet the comet.

Binoculars were lifted to the eyes of the big man and what he saw in the sky brought on an outpouring of childish excitement.

'It's God, be jeepers, that's what it is. It's as if somebody made a hole in the sky and is letting in the light of another world.'

The comet was indeed part of what was going on and, for its time in the sky above us, it seemed to make people happier. People laughed and talked about the strange sight in the darkness of the night and problems seemed to be made smaller and put into the context of the universe.

But maybe Peadar was right. Could it have been the light of another place? The light of the world, another world perhaps?

Christians know the quotation well. It came from the mouth of the God of their understanding ... 'I am the light of the world.'

Here we could see it and feel the effect it was having on the world that we lived in.

'Lord thank you for the comet,' said the Big Man. 'I don't say too many prayers but I want you to know that I am here and therefore I pray. Thank you for the comet and have a good day, Lord.'

THE PASSING OF
A MILLENNIUM

Daniel Mulhall

Daniel Mulhall is the author of *A New Day Dawning: A Portrait of Ireland in 1900*. Born in Waterford he studied at University College Cork and Murdoch University, Western Australia, before joining the Department of Foreign Affairs. Married with two children, he is currently Ireland's Ambassador in Kuala Lumpur.

During the first few days of the New Year, my wife Greta and I threw a party for some close friends. Owing to the time of year, normal dinner-party conversation was abandoned in favour of frivolous games that everyone present thoroughly enjoyed.

In one of these, each guest was secretly assigned the name of a famous figure and had to solve the puzzle by asking questions of the other guests.

The pattern of questioning was remarkably consistent. After clarifying the gender issue, participants invariably tried to pin down the century in which their mystery character had lived. This was fine with remote figures like Napoleon and Marie Antoinette. It somehow did not seem quite right to describe such people as John Lennon, Harrison Ford and Posh Spice as having been born 'in the last century'. However, in the interests of accuracy, it had to be done.

This otherwise inconsequential experience underlines the importance of centuries in the way we process the past. It helped one dinner guest to identify Guy Fawkes when she learned that he had gained notoriety in the seventeenth century. None of those gathered around our dinner table asked if their character had been born during the second Christian millennium, for such information would have been quite meaningless.

We all know that in cosmic terms there is no significance in the passage from one century to another. All of us felt much the same on the first day of January as we had felt during previous weeks and years. And yet, the sense of being in a new era will inevitably reshape the way we see ourselves. We have spent our entire lives referring to the twentieth century as 'this century' and the nineteenth as 'the last century'. As my dinner party guests discovered, that will now have to change. We will have to get used to considering the nineteenth century as a considerably more remote page of our history. As someone with a deep interest in the past, I have repeatedly used the twentieth century as a reliable reference point. My bookshelves are crammed with titles containing the words 'twentieth century'. It was my century, all of our centuries.

It will be some years before books on the 'twenty-first century' begin to be written. Meanwhile, there will, I suppose, be a stronger-than-usual temptation to try to anticipate what the future holds in store. A look back at how people at the turn of the nineteenth century envisaged their future provides a salutary warning against over enthusiastic crystal-ball gazing. They lived in an age of optimism, when economic progress and the success of the European empires in subjugating large parts of the world imbued Europeans with a boundless confidence in their capacity to concoct a rosy future.

No one anticipated the disasters of two world wars, a holocaust or the catastrophes that engulfed Biafra, Bangladesh, Somalia and Rwanda, to name but a few regions devastated by war and famine within living memory. Nor could anything other than science-fiction guesswork have envisioned heart transplants, space travel, strings of chromosomes that determine everything about us and a computer network that rings the globe with more information than has ever been assembled in one place in the history of mankind.

Just like our predecessors a century ago, we have every right to expect science and technology to deliver a benign future, but experience has taught us to beware of double-edged swords and to take nothing for granted.

THE HOGGET

Sylvia Cullen

Sylvia Cullen lives in Co. Wicklow. Her
play *The Thaw* is published by New Island.
NTC toured her most recent commission,
Bedazzled, around Britain and Ireland.

A few years back, one of my research
trips took me to the home of an
elderly man. It was during Lent, so my
biscuits were politely set aside and our
conversation was instead sustained by
strong tea and homemade brown bread.

Of his own accord, the man began
to describe what food meant to him
and all the other labourers as they went
about their work for the big farmer.
Each task was achieved with an
accompanying fantasy, the dreaming
and conjuring up of food. One, as he
milked, would picture a plateful of
salted herrings. Another, doing heavy
work in the stables, called forth

glorified visions of an egg. For himself, the be-all and end-all was 'a meat tea', the mere words alone capable of bringing on a flood of saliva ... It was all too much for the pair of us. More tea had to be made, another square of bread cut and the homemade damson jam spooned thickly over the slices.

Sated, our talk turned and suddenly the room was filled with 'the lads', the Wicklow word for fairies. The man's voice dropped lower and his shoulders shook with giddy laughter. Descriptions flowed of fairy football matches and the dangers of getting them vexed. Take care should I do anything involving a *sceach*, for the lads wouldn't like it – and they'd have ways of letting me know.

Then, a silence came over the room. Something seemed to be bothering the man: his manner changed; he was edgy and unsettled. At last, he announced that he'd have to talk about a certain Christmas ... There had been one particular December when the hunger was fierce. But all eyes were fastened on the twenty-fifth because the big farmer, his father's employer as well as his own, had given a promise to pay money that was owed. The family could put up with a lean, mean month because the prospect of having meat on the table on Christmas Day was a glorious and a joyful one. Agitated, the man moved his blue cup around on its saucer; struggling, he continued describing how Christmas Eve drew near. His father and himself finished all their labours and approached the big man with great hopes ... Tears appeared on the face in front of me before the words could be forced out. 'We got nothing. Only the promise of a hogget. Turned away so we were, out into the bitter cold.' I watched as he relived every step of the way home, crying out his anguish as he described that desolate Christmas table and his parents' sorrow and helplessness, watching their children go hungry. The hogget was never handed over.

When I left the house, I drove around the corner and pulled in, hesitating, weighing up. Not for long. I turned and went back to my previous interviewee, a descendant of that same big farmer.

Straight away she understood, said the man had been on her mind a lot lately, that was why she had recommended him to me. She hadn't been aware of the promise of a hogget but she did know there was some wrong to be righted from way back, explaining that the big man's treatment of his workers had often been less than the best. Before ever I came on the scene, she had already resolved to make some kind of a gesture to the old man. Land, a field, was what she had in mind. And now, after hearing the story of that Christmas more than fifty years ago, perhaps a few hoggets to graze it.

CREAM CAKES

John Trolan

John Trolan was born in Dublin and currently works as Clinical Manager in a rehabilitation unit in Gloucestershire, with a particular research interest in adolescent interventions, particularly amongst the Native American population. He is the author of two novels, *Slow Punctures* and *Any Other Time*

'Tell her to put it on the bill.' I knew as soon as I heard the words that this could be a remarkable solution to all of life's problems, though I couldn't quite believe it. Not until I held the messages in me arms and she had added up the total on a piece of wrapping paper on the counter. 'Me granny said would you put it on the bill?' And out I walked. It was as simple as that. The following morning, I didn't have to be asked. I was up before me granny, waiting to offer to run round to the shops. Haste, or if I have to be common about it, greed, had got me into trouble in the past, so I delayed until I saw how the bill was paid at the end of the week.

'Ask Kathleen how much do I owe her.' And that was that. No more questions asked.

Kathleen was a warm person, but there was something menacing about her. Her irritation hinted this if she had to get off the stool at the counter and walk for something you asked for. Though, as I learned, she was patient about other things. Her hair was always wrapped round spiky pink curlers and held up in a nylon scarf knotted at the top of her forehead. The smoke from a Rothmans, which hung permanently from the corner of her mouth, kept one eye closed. How the ash never seemed to fall from the cigarette is still a mystery. Sometimes, one of her daughters helped out in the shop and Kathleen would sit reading a magazine, resting an ample bosom on stout, folded arms. I'm not saying her breasts were large, but I overheard a rumour at the time that she had to get her brassière on prescription.

When the moment came, I didn't flinch. 'A batch loaf, half dozen eggs ... and a cream doughnut.'

'Does she want the fresh cream or the imitation cream?' she asked, without removing the cigarette. The ash warped, but didn't fall off.

'The fresh cream,' I told her and I pointed at the cream-filled narrow doughnut with a line of jam running along the middle.

I had to scoff it down between one end of Maginns lane and the other. It took longer to clean off the grains of sugar that stuck stubbornly to half of me face. When the bill came at the end of the week, all that was said was, 'I'm sure that oul wan's robbin me.' That's how I discovered that me granny was too proud to question it, but shite floats.

I tried a different cake six mornings a week until fresh-cream slices became me favourite. Two slabs of sweet, caramelised pastry wedged a dollop of cream with a spoonful of jam at its heart. I wasn't so complacent as to refuse the porridge waiting on me when I got back, but I took to eating it out the back yard where we kept a dog who wasn't fussy about things like that.

There's something paralysing about witnessing your own come-uppance, especially when it's quick and unexpected. I walked around the corner of Maginns lane one afternoon straight into me granny and I remember thinking, I'm glad it isn't the morning. I didn't worry, even when she said, 'Come on in to Kathleen's with me and carry a bale of briquettes out to the pram.' Inside, Kathleen leapt down from the stool and her arse started making buttons. Her eyes lit up and she snatched the cigarette out of her mouth.

'Howaya, Annie?'

'Not bad, Kathleen, terrible windy day, isn't it?'

'Yeah, it's blowin' people over out there. How are yeh keepin' anyway?'

'Well, the arthritis is still at me and I can't get rid of this weight I put on. I don't know if it's anthin' to do with the tablets the doctor has me on.'

'Tablets? Sure jaysis, Annie! What about all those cream cakes you're eating?'

CORNER BOYS

Joe Kearney

Joe Kearney was born in Kilkenny in 1951. He worked in the oil industry for over thirty years, before becoming a full-time writer. He has had prize-winning short stories and poems published and is currently working on his first novel.

My grandfather was a corner boy and it skipped a generation before the gift was passed on to me.

He was a man before his time who opted for early retirement from paid labour once he was satisfied that his life's work had been achieved; that was the fathering of nine children. He thereafter pursued a life of voluntary community support. By that, I mean he volunteered to support the gable wall of Moynihan's public house. This establishment was located at the junction of the four streets forming the epicentre of our small midland town and it was from this vantage position that he maintained his watching brief on the comings and goings of the local community.

Where two or more rivers join it's called a confluence. I am convinced that where our four streets converge should be called a conference. I believe this because it was in such a location that my grandfather regularly assembled with his fellow corner boys to confer together, exchange information and comment upon their passive observance of the social and commercial activities of the town. The junction of Green Street, Mill Street, West Street and Chapel Street was commonly referred to locally as 'The Cross'. A low ledge abutted from each of the two public-house windows. One window faced south, the other west, and it was no coincidence that the boys selected these as their preferred crossroads headquarters.

These ledges were of sufficient dimension to comfortably accommodate the backsides of the corner boys and, on warm summer days, allowed them shift position with minimum effort to follow the comfort of the sun's heat. Inclement and winter weather were a different matter, however, and required the adoption of another strategy. A good tweed topcoat and cap were the essential uniform to keep out wind-chill and the worst of the rain. If that failed, they would duck into suitably positioned doorways and by regularly popping their heads out of their shelters were able to follow any unfolding events.

Ireland in the 1950s may have had a slower pace than today. However, sufficient drama was enacted to maintain the boys' interest, punctuate their daily tedium and justify their selfless devotion to this chosen vocation. On fair days there was always the chance excitement of a runaway bullock, maddened by the crowd's clamorous bedlam. More frequently there was the witnessed commotion of a minor motor-vehicle collision or perhaps the accidental fall of a senior citizen or, best of all, the stepping out together of an amorous couple not normally associated together as 'an item'. For days after they would relish the minutia of these events with the same enjoyment as chewing the last tasty morsels from a chop-bone.

Not everyone in the community appreciated their continual visible presence at 'The Cross'. The clergy in particular directed hostile glances at these figures of subversive indolence. My grandfather loved to relate one such encounter with the parish priest. On a Good Friday afternoon, as he was discreetly exiting via the back door of a licensed premises, he had the misfortune to be hotly accosted by the cleric in question with a demand to know if he realised who had died on the cross today. Whipping off his cap, my grandfather dryly replied that he had not been that far down the town and, as such, must have missed all the excitement.

Little did my grandfather and his fellow corner boys realise that they were to impart a legacy to me that would leave a lasting impression on the remainder of my life. I have long since departed that small midland town with its 'conference' of streets, but still find myself in idle moments drawn to pavement cafés, bistros and tavernas that offer street-side seating. There I luxuriate in the indulgence of people watching, keeping the sun on my face, and am always vigilant to the prospect of witnessing, first hand, the enactment of one of life's little minor dramas.

CINEMAS

Gerry McDonnell

Gerry McDonnell is a Dublin poet, playwright and librettist. His latest work is *James
Joyce: Jewish Influences in Ulysses*. He is a
member of the Irish Writers' Union and the
Irish Playwrights' and Screenwriters' Guild.

The cinema is now a place where we
experience movies, respectful and
informed, educated in film studies.
Not so in the fifties! A deafening cheer
rose from the kids as the lights
dimmed and the heavy drapes parted
like the Red Sea. Ushers tried to calm
things down, but another cheer rose
when Abbott and Costello or Laurel
and Hardy appeared.

Some bizarre memories stay with
me. The time the boys from the
industrial school, The O'Brien
Institute, came to the Fairview cinema.
This institution for orphans and other
unfortunates, which provided the

music of the Artane Boys' Band in Croke Park on a Sunday, filled us with dread. The thought that fate could conspire to arrange the unthinkable circumstances whereby we would be sent there terrified and humbled us. Half a dozen rows had been reserved for the boys. The film was *Darby O'Gill and the Little People*. Presumably on the say so of a Brother, the boys opened their packets of Clarnico Murray sweets in unison. The tearing of plastic and unwrapping of sweets drowned out any sound from the screen for at least five minutes.

Some Sunday afternoons we went to 'the Blind', a makeshift cinema in the school for blind boys in Drumcondra, where a Brother operated the flickering projector behind the screen. We sat on wooden benches, albino boys in the front row, and thrilled at the adventures of Zorro and the Lone Ranger; emerging from the dark into the daylight with a blinding headache. The irony of having a cinema in a home for the blind was lost on us.

Back in the real cinemas like the Fairview or the Strand, and more especially in the Savoy and Adelphi in town, the ushers possessed a daunting power. In their impressive uniforms they stood sentinel at the doors to the Promised Land. To be refused admission was equivalent to the social deprivation in being barred from an 'in' pub in adult life. Like barmen, ushers ranged from surly and cranky to welcoming. Dealing with a sometimes-troublesome public, no doubt they had their own side of the story.

Willie Sandford

I finished up Head Usher
in a cinema in town.
That uniform counted for something.
You could bar someone for life.
The cinemas were rough in those days.
It could take three of us
to throw a fella out.

No one knew, but all the time
behind that uniform
I was terrified.
The drink gave me Dutch courage.
I had a right skin-full one night
and didn't see the car coming.

That ended my career as Head Usher.
The uniform was sent back,
blood and muck all over it,
property of the cinema.

Bridie Sandford

My Willie was so proud
of his Head Usher's uniform.
I had my work cut out
keeping it pressed and immaculate.
When he was killed that time
we had a photo of him in it
blown up and framed.
I used to get a laugh
out of visitors
when they saw the photo
and asked,
'Was Willie in the army?'

'No,' I used to say,
'he was in the Adelphi.'

SPADES

Mary Mulvihill

Mary Mulvihill lives in Dublin, where she
works as a science writer and broadcaster.
Her book *Ingenious Ireland*, a celebration of
unsung Irish heritage, won the IBM Science
Journalist of the Year Award in 2003.

Isn't it all too easy to take something
familiar for granted? Take the
humble garden spade, for instance.
Digging the garden last week set me to
thinking about spades. The digging
was hard work, but it would have been
much harder if I had had to dig my
vegetable patch with a small trowel or,
worse, had to scrabble around with
something small and primitive like the
shoulder blade of an ox or even an
oyster shell. Yet those rough tools, if
you can even call them tools, are
probably all that our Stone Age
ancestors had when they started
farming 5,000 years ago.

If it had been me then, I'd have laughed at my farming cousins with their aching backs, and I'd have stuck to being a hunter-gatherer; whereas now that I have a spade, I'm quite happy to dig. For the spade is perfectly designed for its task.

Try it yourself. The sharp metal edge cuts easily and pleasingly through the soil. Thanks to the design of the handle and the footrest, you can put all your weight into the work, digging with your strong leg muscles, rather than exhaust your arms scrabbling about. And then it's an easy matter to use the blade of the spade to lift and turn the sod.

I have only one spade, but a hundred years ago any decent farmer or gardener would have had several spades, each one specially designed for a different task and a particular soil type. There were spades for digging drainage trenches, and scooping spades for cleaning out the drains, and spades for turning sods, and spades for making cultivation ridges. On raised bog, you would use a lightweight foot slane to cut turf; and on blanket bog, where it was easier to get a firm footing, you would use the very different breast slane. And there were numerous other regional variations.

What little I know about spades I have learned from Jonathan Bell, a farming historian who works at the Ulster Folk & Transport Museum near Belfast and who tells me that, amazingly, there were over 1,000 different types of spade in use in nineteenth-century Ireland.

They were made by local blacksmiths and at a few specialised spade mills. Each blacksmith and mill kept the patterns for the spades they made and one spade mill in County Tyrone had 230 different spades in its portfolio. That's the kind of product range that is no longer possible in these days of mass production.

The specialised spade mills needed powerful equipment to drive the massive hammers, rollers and cutters used in working the metal, so most spade mills were around Belfast, Dublin and Cork, where there was a tradition of heavy engineering. Ireland's last traditional spade mill was Patterson's of Templepatrick, a water-powered mill in County Antrim, which closed only in 1990. The National Trust has since restored Patterson's spade mill, and it is again in production. Two spade makers are making turf and garden spades for sale, and this is now the last place in the world where you can buy a hand-crafted spade.

Something to think about next time you dig the garden. And don't call a spade a spade: think of it instead as a sophisticated agricultural implement.

MAKING UP A
FUTURE

Eamonn Kelly

Eamonn Kelly is a Dubliner settled in
Galway, where his first stage plays, *Religious
Knowledge* and *Frugal Comforts*, were prod-
uced. He has worked as a scriptwriter for
RTÉ and in journalism has contributed
articles to various publications, including
The Irish Times.

I now live alone in a centrally heated
flat. It is my home at present, but it
is not home. On good days it is a brief
stopover on a journey to my home
somewhere in the future. On bad days
it is the place I ended up when my
marriage failed.

I spend my time, it now seems,
trying to figure some way of recapt-
uring and repairing the broken past
and plonking the new improved
version into the wide desert spaces of

my future. A futile exercise which only serves to create days of silent regret, building towards an empty future of looking back.

I suppose I could rebuild and renovate that past here and make it more substantial in the telling. Perhaps even succeed in removing all blame from myself. But to do so would only extend the whole sorry story further into my future. So I tick over, bye-byeing the past, waiting for the future to come.

Meanwhile I home as best I can in this centrally heated non-home. Nothing moves but the television images. I stare at them most nights as if they were a fire in a grate, looking in vain for the focus and comfort that a home fire gives.

I need a real fire, real flames. That's what I would do now if I had an open fireplace. I'd get some coal and set the firelighters, lighting them before building the coal around them, leaving the firelighter with space to breath. Soon the coal would be burning and I would down the lights and pull up close to stare beyond the flames into that place where dreams take shape. I would feel the heat of the fire on my face. It is a comforting heat, uneven, too hot on one side, chill on the other, but all the more natural for that. And natural too in the dancing life of the flames darting reflections around the darkened room, creating endless movement and possibility.

And I would stay with the fire until it wanes and casts a warm red glow. The mature fire, perfectly balanced between excitement and collapse. And I would stay with it until the dimmed coals collapsed into the hollow heart of its construction. Then I would rake out the grate, leaving only a bed of glowing coals, and on them I would build the fire anew to witness once again its glorious life and decline. If I had a real fire I might see a future in the flames. If I had a real fire I might feel at home at last.

MUSIC AND SILENCE

WHEN THE WORLD HOLDS ITS BREATH

Paddy Bushe was born in Dublin and lives in Kerry. He writes in Irish and English and has published six books, the latest of which is *Hopkins on Skellig Michael*.

There is a kind of silence when the world holds its breath that is terrifying and that seems to pound around your skull forever, even though it lasts only seconds, or less. The silence on the phone after 'I was speaking to the doctor.' The silence after the screech of brakes behind you. The silence after a boat disappears behind a wave. During the eternity of this silence you wonder will it be broken by the world resuming its normal babbling or by it breaking into a wail. Whether you are experiencing an end or a new beginning. If it is a new beginning, the sound of the world's everyday humming rediscovering itself is as peaceful and regenerative as the deepest quietude and an exhilarating relief from the thunderous silence of the world holding its breath.

I remember one such silence vividly, after almost a quarter of a century. A group of us were walking along a fisherman's path by the bank of the Caragh River at Lickeen, near Glencar, Co. Kerry. It was a bright, boisterous spring day after a few days' storm and rain. I was carrying my infant son in my arms, and my daughter, then two-and-a-half, was walking ahead. It was when she stumbled and fell down the bank that I realised how flooded the river was, how strong the current, how foaming and rocky the channels the water was surging through. I was told afterwards that I laid my son carefully on the ground before jumping down. I have no memory of it; only of the tremendous gasp as the world held its breath over the following seconds. It was those seconds of teetering between life and death that led to this poem, whose title, I hope, will explain itself.

Midwife
for Ciairín

Daughter, that time you fell
From the high bank, in slow
Motion it seemed,
Your two-year-old body turning
Into the black and white
Suddenly loud Caragh River,
And your wide eyes pleaded for breath
Instead of that liquid burning:
That, indeed, was like a little death.

Daughter after my stretched hand
Had slipped – hair floating away –
And slipped again, then grasped, pulled

You, gasping, from the heaving water,
You cried, you were not hurt,
And you were swaddled up
In someone's coat, while the whole earth
Breathed again: o daughter,
That, indeed, was like another birth.

TIME, LIKE AN EVER ROLLING STONE

Mike Absalom

Mike Absalom, until he gave it all up to write books and draw pictures, was an itinerant harpist, puppeteer and song-writer. He now lives and paints near Swinford, Co. Mayo.

If it is true, as I have heard, that the universe is a knotted net of pearls and we are all it and it is all God, then it seems logical to suppose that if I were mischievously inclined enough to untie one of the knots I might stand a chance of finding out something important about the nature of things. And indeed, I once did just that.

When I was a boy, fifty years ago, my father was a country vicar, and it was one of my chores to help him in the parish. At Holy Communion on a

Sunday morning I served at the altar and it was my duty to pump the organ at evensong while he officiated and my mother stumbled through the hymns. There was a little cubbyhole, a kind of tiny second vestry, hidden away behind the stacks of magical silver pipes where I would ensconce myself. It was an enchanted place, lit by thin daylight from a huge leaded window and there was even a pew for me and a thick embroidered hassock.

Evensong, I remember, was often close to sunset, and a particular pale orange light would fall across the back of the wooden organ and at the signal to begin (a loud thumping on the panelling from my mother's side) I would seize the great oar that filled the bellows and pump away two-handed with the vigour of a roman galley slave.

A small lead weight descended on a cord like a slow motion bullet as I pumped and when the bellows was full it stopped and hovered in the air in front of my face. I had time to think then, in that moment of balance, in the orange sunlight, among the flying dust motes, in this holy unseen place, hidden and secure, until the lead weight, now returning to the top of the wall as the bellows emptied, came to a halt, and it was time for me once again to put my shoulder to the oar and pump away.

And if I failed to notice the position of the receding lead, a horrible wail from the organ and the dying gasp of a strangled hymn would call me back to red-faced duty and the apprehension of imminent stern, or at least embarrassing, admonishment.

Each week I made a small mark in pencil on the back of the organ and every fifth week I crossed the marks out and started a new tally.

And one day, there in that orange glow, breathing in the incense of old sun-warmed timber and ancient leather, and making my pencil mark on the back of the organ, the world suddenly stopped dead. I had, not in a blinding flash, but in a crystal clear moment of revelation, a vivid and lasting understanding of the nature of time. The pencil marks might change every week. But the back of the organ did not change. And

Jazz

Micheal O'Siadhail

Micheal O'Siadhail's most recent books
are *Our Double Time: Poems 1975–1995* and
The Gossamer Wall. He has read and
broadcast his poetry widely in Europe,
North America and Japan.

> Are tune and rhythm one in the
> fullness of the play?
> Art Tatum is fingering Someone To
> Watch over Me.
> My jazz, my jazz, will tomorrow be
> my dancing day?

I suppose I'm at a time in my life
when I can look both backwards and
forwards. I'm sure I'm not alone in
wondering how it might have been. If
I'd known better. If I'd taken different
choices. If only. If only. If only. And
yet it was somehow the way I had to
come; this was how my tune unfolded.

Then the looking forward part: dreaming how it will all be. So many wishes, so many desires. And yet in my heart I know that the only thing that's certain is that nothing is certain. Nothing is predictable except that nothing is predictable.

I think this is why I love jazz. It's so full of unpredictability and surprises. If we know anything about how our world works we know that it will surprise us. Any science can describe patterns, how things have developed, tendencies, certain parameters, but there's always the unforeseeable, the unforecastable. Madam Jazz takes up the old battered tunes:

> Someday Sweetheart. Bird of Paradise.
> Nobody Knows. All God's Chillun Got Rhythm.
> Garden of Souls. A Love Supreme.
> Embraceable You. Smoke Gets in Your Eyes

and again fills them with surprise, innovation, renewal, improvisation. *This gaiety where all ends are open-ended.* And I delight in how there's a sort of communal trust between the players, each allowing the other a solo. Each instrument seems to trust implicitly the other. That they both know where they are heading but can never quite know how they'll get there. Madam Jazz blows and drums and fingers, solo and ensemble:

> Before-the-beat, around-the-beat, passion's tone,
> Just on and on swamping up those rhythms,
> Afro, Creole or Latin, the Baptist hymns,
> Even marches, she's making everything her own.

And to think that this music with all its extremes of celebration and melancholy came out of suffering, out of the black slave trade, one of the most tragic chapters in our human history. A music forged in the sweat of cotton-pickers and improvised on a jug and washboard or squeezed out of the banal in Chicago slums. There's some deep sense of acceptance at its heart, as if Madam Jazz lifts all the 'if onlys' of the past and all the dreams of a future into some reckless gaiety:

Keats' kiss-poised lover in my vase of brittle clay
Sings the melancholy of what might but couldn't be.
My jazz, my jazz, will tomorrow be my dancing day?

To know now you wouldn't wish it any other way.
A music bolder in the light of its own fragility.
Are tune and rhythm one in the fullness of the play?

The way it happened I must praise again and say:
What is, what comes, I kiss its sweet uncertainty.
My jazz, my jazz, will tomorrow be my dancing day?

LEARNING TRAD

Mickey McConnell

Mickey MacConnell from Fermanagh is a
journalist and songwriter who has worked
with the *Irish Press* and *The Irish Times*. His
best-known song is 'Only Our Rivers Run
Free' and he now lives in Listowel, Co.
Kerry, and is a columnist with *The Kerryman*.

I'm firmly convinced that few would
argue with me when I say that,
however heroic the attempt, the choice
of Rossini's 'William Tell Overture'
was somewhat unfortunate when, as
two small boys, myself and my brother
Cathal attempted to get to grips with
learning the tin whistle.

Of course it was all my mother's
fault. When she discovered that we had
some little degree of musical talent she
took herself off to Enniskillen and
returned home with a wind-up
gramophone and a selection of old 78

r.p.m. records that she had purchased at not inconsiderable expense in a certain hardware emporium. While this premises may have excelled in all things relating to hardware, when it came to the musical repertoire it left a lot to be desired.

The records mostly featured lugubrious Polish military music played by long-extinct Polish bands, similar fare from the House Bands of numerous British Army regiments, strange and oddly haunting fugues played on a ghostly organ and, of course, Rossini's 'William Tell'. By the time we had mastered all of these my late father, Sandy, and most of the neighbours were at breaking point.

So it was that lengthy letters were written to various musicians all over Fermanagh, Cavan, Tyrone and Donegal, a hackney car hired, a bottle of whiskey purchased and the first of many musical pilgrimages embarked upon. This was no small achievement in those far-off days when cash was scarce and Irish traditional music even scarcer.

Tape recorders hadn't been invented then, or if they were, they certainly were not available to Cathal and myself. Added to that was the unfortunate attitude that all traditional music had to be learned by ear or it could not possibly be the real McCoy. Being musically illiterate, the pressure was on, as we felt it was our sacred duty to return home with at least five or six reels or risk being a disgrace to the family.

So it was that we invented job-sharing. It was agreed that I would concentrate on learning the low parts of the tune, Cathal would concentrate on the 'turn' and if the tune to be learned had more than two parts, then it was a case of the divil take the hindmost. That was the plan and it worked rather well if somewhat erratically.

On the appointed day we would depart in the hackney car and be guided to our eventual destination by reading the numbers from the milk churns which the obliging host would place at strategic locations to direct us up long lanes to the place of learning. It was a method which worked rather well in a time when signposts were few and far between and the rural road network of the northwest was somewhat of a Glorious Mystery.

On arrival the atmosphere was usually fairly formal and strained but would loosen up considerably after Sandy produced the whiskey bottle and poured a few belts for the adult company. Before long the fiddle, flute or melodeon would be produced and the steep learning curve would begin. This involved listening to a tune being played over five or six times and committing it to memory using our brotherly two-step method.

It has to be admitted that the system had its drawbacks. In retrospect I see that most of the musicians we visited were fairly poverty stricken and badly fed. The unfortunate result was that as the whiskey bottle emptied the tunes to be learned seemed to strangely change in character and tempo, sometimes the final result bearing little or no resemblance to the first rendition. However, we quickly learned to adapt and became used to filtering out the alcohol-induced inaccuracies by virtue of comparisons with those versions played before the cork was taken out of the bottle.

And so the first steps of a musical lifetime began. It proved to be a long hard road and sadly one with far too few creamery churns placed at strategic locations to act as solitary landmarks.

CAMPING WITH SCHUBERT

Danny Morrison

Danny Morrison is a former director of publicity for Sinn Féin and an ex-prisoner. He now devotes his time to writing and commentating and has written six books, three of them novels.

The four of us, Leslie, Chrissie, Richard and myself, packed my car with an army tent, sleeping-bags, spare clothes, food and drink and headed off on a camping holiday, to be out of the North and away from everything.

In some ways I was trying to retrace the summer of 1971 when my friend Noel and I hitched around the west of Ireland. It was four weeks before the introduction of internment and the opening of a 'temporary' prison camp called Long Kesh. It was very difficult being eighteen against the backdrop of increasing conflict; it was very difficult remaining neutral.

But away we went – Noel in search of the source of traditional Irish music, I, angst-ridden and serious as usual, in search of answers to the bewilderment of life. I insisted we take no tent, so we slept out in the open: on benches in Galway; in a bog just outside Oughterard, where the countryside was bare and lonely and the wind was high in the sky and whistling: and, later, when Noel found more companionable drinking partners in Bundoran, I wandered alone around the town after midnight, before making my way up the cliff path beside the golf course and bedding down in a small shelter.

That next morning I rose at dawn, hungry and thirsty and shivering, and walked to the top of the cliff and looked out over the Atlantic. I became detached yet, I thought, why am I always *here*, and a unique contentment came over me as I sat at the edge of the world and watched a lone beam break through the clouds and travel to the water. I was so happy and I cried to God for allowing me experience the thrill of life.

When I returned seventeen years later my youth had long disappeared and I was far from innocent.

Our women hated the tent, imagined an invasion of snakes and tarantulas and only the bribe of a half bottle of brandy each night could persuade them not to desert us for a B & B. In Galway, when Chrissie phoned home to find out how her three kids were, I went into a shop and bought a cassette tape of Schubert's Fifth Symphony.

We decided to head southeast – to the fleadh in Kilkenny. My three exhausted companions – we had almost been swept away in gale-force winds in Tulla Cross the night before – fell asleep as I drove.

An abbreviated version of the second movement of Schubert's Fifth was once used as the theme for a film or children's TV programme about these kids who find a secret door in the wall surrounding a mysterious garden, through which they enter and have great adventures before they go home. But one day they can't find the secret passage, and they feel desolated and are conscious that something has changed or been lost forever.

As I drove, the music filled me with immense pleasure and I stole a glance at my girlfriend, head tilted back, in dreamland, and appreciated how lucky I was, how peaceful and kind those few days had been, even with the storm. Later, we were all agreed that we had had such a great time that we would make the same trip again, but other things intervened and we never did, and probably never will.

But for a few moments, at the wheel of my car, driving out of Galway and through the Irish countryside, I felt I had found that secret door in the wall and glimpsed the various gardens of innocent adventure I had once known, felt that I was once again watching that lone beam strike the ocean, telling me how alive and lucky I was.

THE REST IS SILENCE

Noirín Ní Riain

Noirín Ní Riain is an internationally
acclaimed singer from Co. Limerick. She
has recently been awarded a Doctorate in
Theology from the University of
Limerick. The heart of her research she
calls 'theosony', which is towards a
theology of listening.

In the amazing world of music,
silence and sound are soulmates.
One depends on the other. The rest is
music. The rest is silence.

Yet, like a good human relationship, both remain other and enhance
one another in the perfect balance and
tension inevitable for the song or piece
of music to spread its wings and fly.
Silence is the sacred space out of
which music weaves its way in and
through our aural world. An interval of

silence is appropriately called a 'rest' in music, a time of refreshing quiet.

Aldous Huxley, the British novelist, wrote: 'After silence that which comes nearest to expressing the inexpressible is music.'

The art of the rest/silence envelopes the inevitable trinity of actors in the drama of music: firstly, there's the composer; secondly, the performer/conductor; and finally, you, the sympathetic listener.

I use the word 'sympathetic' carefully. It's well-source is from the mellifluous ancient Greek language. *Patheia* means feelings or emotions and *sympatheia* puts a word on co-sharing, sharing these feelings with one another.

The composer is the midwife – the very source of the music – the god/goddess of the river of sound, just as Sionna is the source and goddess of this magical Shannon River beside me. The composer is reaching out for the perfect tune, finding the elusive equipoise between silence and resonance. And that resonance can offer incredible possibilities which, again, like silence, can mirror the measure of one's imagination.

It is this drive or inspired vision which spans time and timbre from, on the one hand, the precise measured silences of the Bachean *Brandenburg Concertos* to the innovative compositions by the late contemporary composer John Cage, such as *4.32*, on the other.

Bathed in silence again, the music remains invisible and still in the mind of the composer or on the silent page of manuscript waiting its moment to sing its song.

Then the performer is the one who strikes the bell of sound. But the heart of this sounding is yet another dance with silence – as the ancient Chinese proverb goes, 'the midnight when noon is born'. At that very point, the silence is broken and explodes on the universe of listeners like the Big Bang of Music.

William Stafford, the Kansas poet, captures that transformative life of the imagination. This poem, incidentally, he wrote on 10 August 1993, just eighteen days before he died.

A shudder goes through the universe, even
long after. Every star, clasping its
meaning as it looks back, races outward
where something quiet and far waits.
Within, too, ever receding, into its fractions,
that first brutal sound nestles closer
and closer toward the tiny dot of tomorrow.
And here we are in the middle, holding
it all together, not even shaking.
Hard to believe.

The Julian
Meetings

John Wakeman

John Wakeman has a second book of poems, *A Sea Family*, due out in 2005. He founded *The Shop: A Magazine of Poetry* in 1999 and has edited major reference books on literature and film.

My wife Hilary is a rector in the Church of Ireland. Before that she was a vicar in the Church of England. But long before she was ordained, she did a remarkable thing.

A great vogue for meditation began all over the West in the 1960s. Some took it up because a bit of the old meditation was held to improve your performance at business meetings, or in bed, but most because they were looking for inner peace, or enhanced self-knowledge, or some other spiritual benefit that doesn't come with the capitalist religion. They adopted various systems of Buddhist meditation, yoga meditation, transcendental meditation, meditation taught by all kinds of eastern mystics and gurus.

What few seemed to be giving much heed to was the great tradition of Christian meditation. This troubled Hilary, who by the beginning of the 1970s had already seized upon that tradition. Having abandoned organised religion in her late teens, she'd come back to it years later and, as she puts it, 'had rediscovered the wordless and imageless' prayer of her childhood. She thought the Christian churches should be making some provision for people like her, but none of the church leaders she approached had anything to offer. So she wrote a letter that was published in the *Church Times*, the *Catholic Herald* and several other such papers.

Her letter proposed an association of Christians of all denominations who, while remaining in their homes and jobs, would come together from time to time to practise contemplative or mystical prayer. Within a couple of weeks, she received letters from 166 people who wanted to know more.

She picked out a few individuals in selected population centres around the UK and asked them for a meeting and a bed for the night. One morning in May 1973, she dumped our five kids in my reluctant lap and headed off. By the end of the year, she'd set up a dozen groups devoted to contemplative prayer and loosely affiliated with the organisation she and a few of her friends had created. They called themselves the Julian Meetings, after the English mystic Julian of Norwich. It was she who famously predicted that 'all shall be well, and all manner of things shall be well'. And they have been – at least for the Julian Meetings. It now has nearly 500 groups in nine countries, including a few in Ireland.

What is silent contemplative prayer? I'm not exactly the best person to answer that question. Silence makes me jumpy. I'm not even a believer, though I'm less militant around Christians like

Hilary. They'll forgive you as soon as they look at you, and that's very galling.

Hilary herself, in *Circles of Silence*, a book about the Julian Meetings, says that contemplative prayer is a 'stilling of the mind and body to attend to God'. How do you still your mind? Well, I know that our brains give off electrical impulses that can be measured. When we're thinking hard, working away to deal with the world around us, these impulses are fast and frequent. In silent contemplation, apparently they slow right down. You go into a state of what's called 'relaxed awareness', in which you forget the outside world and turn your attention inward. As I understand it, or misunderstand it, it's in the silence of their own innermost beings that some people feel most in touch with God.

T.S. Eliot refers to this in his late sequence of poems *Four Quartets*. He talks about something he calls 'the still point of the turning world', where there is: 'The inner freedom from the practical desire/the release from action and suffering, release from the inner/And the outer compulsion, yet surrounded/By a grace of sense, a white light still and moving.'

I left the Church of England when I was sixteen, and I don't expect I'll return. For that reason, it makes me uneasy to be talking about things like divine grace. But I'm more comfortable with them in poems than in prayers. I suppose I get from poetry a substitute for what Hilary gets from her faith.

MARY OVER
MINERVA

William Wall

William Wall has published three novels
and two volumes of poetry, most recently
Fahrenheit Says Nothing to Me. His fourth novel,
This Is the Country, is published in 2005.

A butterfly has no internal source of
body-heat but needs actual
sunlight to quicken his muscles: hence
butterflies rarely pass through shadow
but take their uneven course from one
bright place to another. A man is both
more adaptable and less fortunate,
troubled by darkness but unable to
tolerate the light forever.

If you find yourself in Rome and
the sun glares in fury from a sky that is
perpetually cobalt blue, as it will do,
there is always the church. There are, in
fact, as somebody once said to me, too
many churches in Rome.

But it is a serene experience to walk out of the warm sun, sit on a bench by way of catching your breath and resting your feet, and find yourself gazing for several minutes, in mute astonishment and without recognising it, on a statue made by Michelangelo.

This happened to me in the beautifully named church of Santa Maria Sopra Minerva – Holy Mary over the Goddess Minerva.

Fate, as someone said, conspires with the well-disposed traveller to send him the very things he is bound to love.

I retrace my steps now, like a film rewinding and beginning again at a critical juncture. I walk off the sunlit Piazza Venezia, tired perhaps by the crowds of young people who sit under the trees with their backs toward Trajan's column and their faces to the sun and the crazy traffic. I walk along the Via del Plebiscito, through the Piazza Gesù and finally into the Piazza Minerva.

Already I am grateful to that goddess, for the side of the square on which I walk is blessedly shaded.

A little off the Piazza is a foolish-looking dome on a rather plain building. There is little evidence that it might be a church until I notice that the door is open. I am drawn inwards by the promise of darkness.

Galileo prayed here during his interrogations by the Inquisition. I hear his cork-heeled sandals creaking in the apse. There is the Michelangelo *Redeemer*, just one of a number of striking sculptures. There are Lippi frescoes to feed the soul and confound the heart.

In my mind's eye I see a master painter working against time with his tiny patches of wet plaster, watching the paint softening and being absorbed, knowing that just such work had elsewhere already lasted a thousand years and wondering what, in a thousand more, men would think of his.

Or is he so absorbed by the effort of reconciling each brush-stroke with the great conception of the whole that nothing occupies his thought except the behaviour of the last square inch of colour?

Or Michelangelo trying to anticipate what truth would emerge from the marble under his hand: what unexpected triplet of pain, piety and beauty to trouble his dreams?

Months later I am still thinking about it – and about the amazing good fortune that brought me there, out of the sun and into the silence, in Santa Maria Sopra Minerva, on a warm day in Rome.

SILENCE

Michael Harding

Michael Harding has written two books of fiction and numerous plays for the Abbey Theatre and other Irish theatre companies.

It's not that we want silence so much. It's more that we are afraid of noise. We are trying to get away from noise. Silence is a refuge from something else. Silence is the absence of things.

I remember in childhood silence was the absence of argument. Argument was the colour in the sky. The unhappiness of things. Craving for sweets. Fighting over toffee bars. Dissatisfaction with football matches. With table-tennis bats.

And the arse kicked in the schoolyard. The fights. Rows. Boxing matches. The rude teachers. The belt and cane. The Irish verbs. The dot over the C in the words for 'I saw the man'

— *chonaic mé fear*. The ferocity of grammar. What is the answer? You. *Seas suas*.

And then there was the argument of adults. About lawns. Dogs. Newspapers. Golf clubs.

The confusion of childhood was followed by the secondary school where there was a gang. Two or three boys. Bullies. They roamed the corridors and the basements and the showers and the toilet area and the landings to the dormitories. Frightening people. Stopping smaller boys for questioning. Demanding cigarettes. Information. Radios. Humiliating them. Come here. Stand there. Don't look at me like that.

They shoved fists into little chins. Pushed the back of the head against the wall.

No one stopped them. No one chastised them. Far from it. The bullies were at the top of the tree for praise. Little boys were laughed at.

I saw many boys from secondary school go through the rest of their lives struggling with alcoholism, depression and anger at having been treated so brutally.

A number of boys I knew committed suicide as adults. One jumped out a window. One walked into a lake. One dived off a balcony.

Did the terrors of childhood trigger off some interior argument? An inner bully of the mind that never let them go. Still hunted after all those years. Still terrorised and craving silence in their hearts

In order to find silence as a boy, I went fishing. The reel and the line and the little voblex bait tossed on the brown lake. Flat water at evening time. Midges. Geese on the far shore. But the fish didn't like it. They looked at me with their mouths full of hooks. I tried battering their heads off the stones once or twice, but it produced an uneasy feeling in the pit of my stomach. And sometimes when the fish didn't bite I felt angry with them.

Bite, I hissed. Bite yis dirty fish. I found my hands gripping the rod too tightly.

Pulling the line too harshly when the bait got lodged behind a stone in the water.

Cursing when the line broke. Cycling off in rage. I noticed that the argument had taken root inside me.

Fish are easy to catch. Silence is a different kettle. A hard thing to find.

To make all the arguments fall away. To make all the voices still. The clenched fist that shouts at the pike.

I long for the refuge of silence. When there is no argument.

ON NOISE AND SPEED

Kerrie Hardie

Kerrie Hardie grew up in Co. Down and now lives in Co. Kilkenny. Her poems have won many prizes and her publications include *A Furious Place* (1996) and *Cry for the Hot Belly* (2000). Her first novel, *Hannie Bennet's Winter Marriage*, also appeared in 2000; another, *The Bird Woman*, is forthcoming.

These days, more and more, I forget what I am, what I know. I go through my life keeping up, tensing with effort, falling further and further behind.

Around us technology soundlessly, seamlessly proliferates. Communication moves faster and further, daily we become more accessible to each other, speak more, hear more, see more; the air thickens with words, music throbs in our ears, images beat down the

• 268 •

doors of our eyes, blurring out vision with brightness and colour and speed.

No one forces us. We voluntarily enrol ourselves.

This is the way of it: I am willing, I do my best, I strain, learn, keep up, I am effortfully being whatever it all requires of me.

But for myself, I can't do it for very long. For a moment I am suspended, a stone held over a well. Then I am dropped.

Stone, falling through air for a long time, breaking through water, sinking downwards into its depths.

I am immobile, defeated, at rest. This is failure. I remember again about being slow – that my nature is slow. I remember that when I am slow I can listen, that when I am slow I can hear. Everything. Even silence.

I give up and listen. I talk less, write slow letters, sit on steps. The more I listen, the more I hear. I hear the whole world, it comes to me effortlessly, air moving through an open window.

Here is a poem about allowing silence.

Communication

My father won't talk on the telephone.
He hands it to my mother,
then tells her what to say to me.
He seems to need this go-between. As though without,
I am too raw – the whole complicated business
too risky, too much effort. My brother is the same,
preferring answerphones. I am less sure.
I think I have to do these things – I prise myself loose
from my nature. Sometimes after a long call, I feel betrayed
into words I have not thought through, accused because
I do not want this miracle.
I am too slow to move so fast.
Alone in the house, I let the phone ring for days.
I don't turn on stereo or radio or television.
The membrane of the walls thin like muslin, the light

presses through. Wind sounds, bird sounds,
field sounds of cattle and sheep,
penetrate. The swish of crows flowing over.
I live deep in the world.
I grow like my father.

INEVITABILITY
OF THE CAR

Brendan Lynch

Brendan Lynch turned to journalism after being imprisoned for anti-Nuclear activities. A former racing cyclist and driver, he has written two books and contributed to such media as *The Observer* and *The Irish Times*.

The arrival of the motorcar was inevitable. As far back as the thirteenth century, scientist Roger Bacon wrote of the day when we would endow chariots with increased speed, without the aid of any animal.

By the 1890s, the bicycle had given the public a foretaste of the exciting possibilities of individual long-distance transportation. It also helped to break down social barriers and particularly fostered a growing independence among women.

Leading characters in books by H.G. Wells used the bicycle as an aid to social mobility.

By the turn of the century, no fewer than ten million Americans owned their own personal wheels. The world was ready for the automobile, whatever the price yet to be paid – millions of fatalities, unholy oil wars and the merry despoliation of city and countryside alike.

Automobile defenders pointed out that previous means of transport had their own dangers. Many perished in railway mishaps, while hundreds were killed each year in accidents involving horses. Two outside passengers were frozen to death in 1812 on the Bath to Chippenham coach.

Horses were blamed for the spread of disease, particularly eye and intestinal infections among children. With each animal producing an estimated forty-five pounds of dung daily, Londoners had to tip a crossing sweep to clear a path through odoriferous and fly-infested streets. The clatter of hooves and metal wheels frequently made conversation impossible. Automobile supporters insisted that not only would the time-saving cars be cheaper to run than horses, they would also be cleaner and safer.

The parents of the petrol-engined car were the Germans Karl Benz and Gottlieb Daimler, who produced the first petrol-engined vehicles in 1886. The big advantage of petrol over steam-powered cars was that they required only one kind of fuel, instead of a combination of coal and water. They were also ready to work as soon as they were started! Many big stores soon replaced their horses with motorised vans, each of which could more speedily do the work of three horses.

Growing increasingly more reliable and simpler to use, the car soon grew more popular. But it was some time before it was to be completely acceptable socially. When one early motorist visited his father, he was requested to bring a container to catch the oil drops. 'Certainly, father,' he replied, 'if you will bring a bigger one for your carriage horses when you next visit me!'

It was the 1903 Gordon Bennett motor race that finally established the car in Ireland. But the car's appearance still caused consternation in rural areas. Two Kilkenny schoolgirls bolted in terror from 'dem divils on wheels' when English motorists asked for directions.

Another automobile caused Wexford's first recorded extraterrestrial sighting – and simultaneously reiterated the power of Faith. An elderly woman who had never seen a car before was on her way to market, when she was overtaken by pioneer motorist, John Magrath. As she recovered from shock in town, she related how she had seen a carriage from the other world, with a horribly ugly demon driving it.

'I knew he was coming to take me to hell but I made a sign of the cross. And when I looked again, thanks be to God, he had vanished in a cloud of dust!'

THE TYRANNY
OF SPEED

Michael Cronin

Michael Cronin was born in Dublin and is currently Director of the Centre for Translation and Textual Studies at Dublin City University. He was co-editor of *Graph* cultural review from 1986 to 1999. His *Time Tracks: Scenes from the Irish Everyday* was published by New Island in 2003

In 1900, there were fewer than two thousand transactions per minute on the New York Stock Exchange; now there are one million. Moore's Law dictates that the speed of personal computers doubles every eighteen months or less. Acceleration is the new religion of modernity. David Hancock, chief of the Hitachi Corporation's portable computer division, encouraged his workers to greater productivity with the slogan,

'Speed is God and time is the devil.' To be on the move is to be on the make and to be on the make is to be on the way up. As the advertisement showing an old manual telephone exchange puts it, 'Stand still and you're history.' Like Aladdin's carpet, even the office itself must rise up and float into a paradise of pure mobility, the telephone and the laptop and the digital assistant freeing the users from their earthly attachments as they join the chorus of digital angels watching over our global economy.

We usually measure speed in units of impatience not achievement. It is when we are stuck in traffic that we start comparing ideal drive time to the agonisingly slow reality of gridlock. It is when the World Wide Web becomes the World Wide Wait that we grow impatient at slowness and want our machines to work even faster. In these moments of fretful anxiety, we sense that we have become accustomed to a level of speed that would startle earlier generations. Familiarity breeds discontent. We want quicker service, quicker access, shorter download times. Increasingly, our shops and our city streets and our roads reflect the urgent imperatives of acceleration. Night is no longer a period of rest, Sunday no longer a harbour of stillness. Twenty-four hours a day, seven days a week, employees service our relentless appetite to consume. In medieval Christendom, religious festivals and feast days were a break from the frenzy of the everyday. Lent and advent were times set apart, times for slowing down and reflection. But now that we no longer distinguish sacred time from secular time, there are increasingly few moments of deceleration in our lives, no checks on the dizzy spin cycle of consumption. Like exhilarated but frightened children at the fairground, are we beginning to feel disorientation and nausea, wanting to come down from the chair-o-plane of late modernity but not sure how?

Speed kills and time is its first victim. The faster our cars go, the more miles we travel in them. The cars may be more powerful but the tailbacks into the cities are longer. As people move around faster and faster, it becomes harder and harder to meet them. They spend less and less time in more and more places. A few minutes here, a snatched conversation there, are the precarious rewards of velocity. The leisure society is not a hope for the future but a thing of the past.

If speed has become the new God, perhaps slowness is the ultimate heresy. When revolutionary change is discussed in science or industry or politics, the language is often saturated with the dizzy rhetoric of speed: the race to discover the new drug, the dramatic cuts in production cycles, the sudden unleashing of radical new forces in the society. Even dissent works with a stopwatch. Perhaps, what we need is not to mobilise but to demobilise, to disconnect, to argue for the radical insights of deceleration. The age of the soundbite fears deliberation, the complex, patient search for truth. Better it seems the glib platitudes of the fast thinker than the painstaking enquiry of human beings who are aware only of their uncertainties and that anything worth knowing or cherishing makes huge, unconditional demands on our time. Hurtling down our own information superhighways, we may pride ourselves on forgetting the past but will we remember that we too are mortal and that our futures should not be endlessly compromised by the time-to-market tyranny of real time?

FAITH

COMPASS

Eamon Morrissey

Eamon Morrissey, born in Dublin, has acted and written for theatre, television and radio, at home and abroad, for over forty years. Married to Ann for almost as long, he is still enjoying life.

I have a little pocket compass that has been a great help to me on misty, unfamiliar hills, but nowadays whenever I take a plane journey I try to remember to bring it with me. Now I know, in a modern, fly-by-wire, computerised Airbus, it is a bit ludicrous for me to be sitting there consulting my boy-scout-type compass, and indeed cabin crew do find it amusing. But the compass has a purpose. It is a remnant, a relic if you like, of the time when I sought to come to terms with an awful phobia, a fear of flying, which I developed. I sympathise with anybody who has a phobia of any kind. They are dreadful things. The world and your own reason can tell you that you are being silly, but exposed to the phobia, your mind and body fill with a terrible fear and panic, and to be free of my own phobia about flying was a wonderfully liberating event in my life. The pocket compass remains with me as a sort of talisman, but nowadays it has a more positive use, for it helps me to be aware of the experience of the journey itself.

For our ancestors, crossing the Atlantic in frail sailing ships was a massive and often dangerous journey. When steam arrived those uncomfortable, dangerous weeks at sea were replaced by just six days. Now we cross that vast ocean in six hours. But the extent of the journey is the same, the same great half circle as we follow the curvature of the earth. Of course, in a jet it is hard to get a sense of the extent of that journey. Today we are inclined to measure travel in time rather than distance. The destination, the arrival time, is the important thing. The journey itself becomes a sort of non-place between two cities. Rather than being on a journey, we are 'in transit'. And that is a pity.

Now, I have no wish ever to be forced to travel in a leaky three-master across the Atlantic, although at the height of my fear of flying I would have preferred it. One time, we did return from America by ship, and although it was a good experience, for me once was enough. I am happy to get there, or back, in six hours, but to give me some sense of being on a journey, and not in a non-place, not 'in transit', is where my little compass comes in. It will not tell me exactly where I am at any given moment but it shows me the direction in which I am heading and, at the very least, that makes me aware that I am on a journey.

Now and again, I find myself thinking about my own journey through life, and I wonder for how much of that journey was I simply 'in transit', just getting from point A to point B in my life as quickly as possible. Although at times it can be scary, at least that journey of life does not fill me with fear and panic, and I am glad of that. But I begin to see, and regret, that there were parts of that life journey I embarked upon without even the guidance of a boy-scout compass.

THE DARK HOPE

Enda Wyley

Enda Wyley was born and lives in Dublin. She has published three collections of poetry, *Eating Baby Jesus* (1994), *Socrates in the Garden* (1998) and *Poems for Breakfast* (2004).

The feather blows out of the flats, its strange colours flapping brightly. It's a magic feather. The children wish they could live in a different place. They know that if they catch this feather they can make a wish on it and their dream will come true. So, they race down the steps and out into the bright day, the feather dancing above their heads, leading them on. This is the beginning of a story I made up for children in Fatima Mansions as part of a creative-writing workshop I ran for them.

In the story, the children chase after the feather. It stops over a group of adults and children planting bulbs near the crèche; it moves on to the community centre, where other children are making butterfly wings for a parade, painting their faces bright and singing newly learnt songs.

The children in the story stop to watch all these activities and then run on after the feather as it passes a group of majorettes in their blue outfits, their hair scraped back into tight buns, rehearsing for a show. Then as the feather moves out onto the training field the children race after it to find a football team being coached for a league match.

The children never catch the feather. But slowly they realise that where they live isn't so bad after all, that their wish has, in fact, always been there around them. Maybe when the children walked home after the workshop they thought about the magic feather and the different things it flew past in the story. Maybe they began to realise that the place they live in is not so different to that in the story.

In the places we least expect, hope can often raise its head and we are startled – as if we have pulled aside shutters in a dark room and felt light surprisingly fall like diamonds on a black winter floor. On Sean McDermott Street before Christmas I remember how a priest blessed a new sculpture at the junction of Buckingham Street.

We remembered the dead – those who had succumbed to Aids in the decay of the surrounding streets and flats. I thought of one woman in particular, who in the last few weeks of her life had only one wish in mind – to get married and to be driven around Stephen's Green in a horse-drawn carriage. We all at some point in our lives have stood at a difficult junction, realising the bleakness of our situation but somehow have looked up to hope, like a brave man splattering blessings far out across the street with holy water – love's unexpected gifts.

And suddenly you are on a busy street corner, lost in thought, about to innocently step out into the wild sea of traffic and to lose your life – but a stranger's hand reaches from behind, pulls you so quickly back that you do not have time to think.

Love, the dark hope, not wanting to be thanked or noticed, moves on in the crowd and is nameless, faceless. The room fills with light again and you are, in a split second, saved.

DEEP ECOLOGY
AND THE OAK
TREE

Dick Warner

Dick Warner is a writer, broadcaster and environmentalist. He is a former RTÉ radio producer and has written and presented many television documentaries. He lives in rural Co. Kildare.

I have become interested in the ideas of an eccentric Norwegian thinker called Arne Naess. He called his philosophy 'Deep Ecology'. Some of the ideas are rather complicated and I don't fully understand them. But I'd like to give you a feel for how Deep Ecology works.

Imagine you are walking in a wood. It's an old wood of native oaks. You come to a little clearing in the wood and you sit down on a mossy rock for a rest. You are looking idly at a large oak tree on the other side of the clearing. What, you wonder, can I say with any authority about that tree? Well … I can say that it is a separate living organism, just as I am. And I can say, rather more obviously, that I can see the tree but it can't see me.

Deep Ecology would question both of these statements.

Let's take the simpler one first. Undoubtedly you can see the tree, but are you quite sure the tree can't see you? To be able to see you have to be sensitive to light. And there are few living things more light sensitive than oak trees. When that oak breaks dormancy at the end of winter all the processes – the initial rising of the sap from the roots to the top-most twigs, the final bursting of the buds and unfolding of the leaves – are controlled by day length. So that tree is not only deeply sensitive to light, it can also measure the amount of it in a day with more precision than you can without instruments.

For trees, life in a forest is a battle for light. They grow away from the shade, reaching for the sun. Oh yes, that oak tree can see you, probably better than you can see it, and it can also see your shadow. It may not understand what it sees, but then I too see many things that I don't understand.

Now let's go to that other assumption. You are a single living organism and so, separately, is the oak tree. Not really. The more we get to understand nature, the more we realise that the real organism is the forest. The forest is an incredibly complicated system that works through networks of fungal mycelia stretching like nerves through the leaf mould, by complex hierarchies of insects, birds and mammals, by a finely balanced rhythm of birth and death. It's a machine designed to serve the true monarchs of creation – the bacteria. The oak tree is only one cell in that organism. And, of course, while the oak may live for centuries, the forest is potentially immortal. A strong point in its favour, in evolutionary terms.

And take you, that body and soul sitting on a damp, mossy rock. Are you sure you are an individual organism? Maybe you are just a colony of little organisms, of bacteria and funguses and individual cells, all with their jobs to do. Maybe you are just an ants' nest or a beehive. Or are you a forest?

It's interesting stuff, this Deep Ecology.

THE ANATOMY
OF SILENCE

Macdara Woods

Macdara Woods was born in 1942 and is
married to Eiléan Ní Chuilleanáin. With
Leland Bardwell and Pearse Hutchinson,
they are founder editors of the literary
review *Cyphers*. He has published ten books
of poems and edited *The Kilkenny Anthology*.
He is a member of Aosdána.

Archaeology is concerned with
absences, deals not so much with
the dead as with the present and the
absent. Construing the evidence of
absence is where human fallibility and
carelessness, and sometimes worse,
come into it. The science of hype and
sound bite, spin and gloss – do we
simply not notice what we are saying,
for example, when we speak of people
being made redundant? How many
people are lost to history every day,
cropped from photographs, stories

edited from the text, even as the newspaper or magazine or instant book-about is being put together for the edgy readers?

And if we can declare the living redundant, what chance the absent dead? Do sound bite, spin and gloss hold as much dominion in that democracy as they do for the rest of us? I ask because when I stopped-by at the graveyard in Inniskeen, last January, to pay my respects to Patrick Kavanagh, I found that although his name is clearly indicated, along with quotations from his work, as is perfectly right and proper, somehow the name of his wife, Katherine, who is buried beside him, has been erased from the precincts, as if she had never been. There used to be an inoffensive headstone, of the ordinary Irish graveyard kind, with both their names upon it, but this, according to report, was broken up and thrown into a local boggy field.

Sin mar a bhíonn, bfhéidir, but I knew them both and Katherine was a decent, caring, warm-hearted, generous woman, who loved and looked after Patrick in the last decade of his life, and to whom she was married in her family's parish church, the Church of the Three Patrons, in Rathgar, in Dublin, in 1967. It is not proper, nor tolerable surely, that she should be denied the right to have her name on a headstone, beside that of her husband, marking the grave in which they are both buried.

I can scan the landscape in Umbria, or Ireland, because it is still being written, inscribed, by the people who have inhabited and worked it from before writing itself. I could not properly scan the landscape in South Missouri, a landscape of great and now protected beauty, partly, I think, because the people who had originally left their bones there were gone. Their writing of the landscape interrupted, broken off.

Last June I visited Berlin, a city where presence and absence are immediate and superimposed, terrible histories and peoples present through their absence. How, in the end, can the missing be recorded? To remember the millions propelled beyond memory into nothingness. It's argued, even, if it could be done at all, or should be, what mark – if any – might be appropriate. What monument would not be offensive? And I don't know, but I think in Berlin it is happening; and it is happening through art, in the urban perspectives of the collective mind, like the inscribing of the landscape by those who live in it.

The sculpture in Koppenplatz, for instance – a bronze table and two chairs, one chair upright, the other disturbed, thrown over on its side; or the Missing House in the Grosse Hamburger Strasse – an empty space with the names of those who had lived there on plaques on the party walls of the adjoining houses; or finally – say – Micha Ullman's window in the cobbles in Bebelplatz, just off the Unter den Linden, the site of the Nazi book-burning in 1933. When you look down through the window, you look into a doorless room, a white cell, filled from floor to ceiling with empty shelves and nothing more, and then you notice a small plaque set into the ground with the quotation from Heine's play *Almansor*, from 1820, lines spoken by a Spanish Moslem: 'Wherever they first burn books they will also burn people too, in the end.'

OUT FAR,
IN DEEP

Mark Granier

Mark Granier's poems have appeared in numerous outlets both here and in the UK. He published his first collection *Airborne* in 2001 and he won the Vincent Buckley Poetry Prize in 2004.

As I write this I'm parked at the end of a certain cul-de-sac in Sandycove. Before me is a low granite wall. Beyond it, a crumpling of big rocks like ancient, brown wrapping paper. Then that pristine, unreal estate, changeless, but with change written all over it. It is four o'clock on a December evening, a few weeks before Christmas. The sea has already shifted from scratched turquoise to battered pewter, darkening by the minute. I've just spotted a seal, bobbing blackly beyond the rocks. Further out, the full scoop of Dublin Bay, with its measure of infinity, is made intimate by the drowsy, protective embrace of Howth trailing a glimmer of lights.

Another car has pulled up, engine idling, radio on full blast. Thankfully the windows are closed. The DJ's babbling is muffled, a bass swarm in a jam jar. This is a popular view. A car may dock and depart every twenty minutes or so. None will linger as long as I do. Not many would have the inclination to let this view work on the mind, a vessel for clouds, oncoming night, the returning undertow of memory.

Half four. Howth has melted into an ash-grey cloudbank. A gust of wind, bristly with rain, buffets the car. What I took to be a seal has revealed itself just now as a rubber-suited diver, masked, head down, doing a leisurely crawl past my windshield. A snorkeller? Looking for what, in this failing light, under that restless, inscrutable surface?

Of the beach-going crowd, Robert Frost wrote:

They cannot look out far.
They cannot look in deep.
But when was that ever a bar
To any watch they keep?

Of course, Frost may have been aligning this 'look' with another horizon, as the word 'watch' suggests. And technically, he's right about not being able to look out far. At sea level, after only a few miles our planetary curve severs all lines of sight as surely as a blade. But those miles are marvellously unobstructed. The watcher's gaze is given leave to sweep, dive, soar or perch on a big container ship, stationary as an oilrig. Then you glance up after only fifteen minutes and it's over the line, history.

I've grown used to knowing the sea is there. Not far off, behind the props of bricks, glass, trees. Off to the side. A blue zone, to complement what's left of our green one, the soft graph of the Dublin Mountains. My need to look at the sea is easily assuaged. My dependence requires only that I find, every now and then, somewhere like this cul-de-sac and stay long enough for the mind's restless, cluttered eye to find its counterweight. There is something of this equilibrium to be found in any waterway – the banks of the Grand Canal in Dublin, for instance, where Patrick Kavanagh underwent what he described as his spiritual birth. Something in the rhythm and play of light on water keeps us watching. Keeps us hopeful.

It's after five now, deepening to nightfall. The frog-person is out of the picture. I'm looking at two broad bars of blue, the upper one slate, the lower one almost lead. Hard to see any movement, except when the darker bar splits into creamy ruffles on three turf-dark rocks. I'll be going soon. I've almost had my fill. A good, sloshing bucket-full, which I can take home and place on whatever mental scales registers these things.

IT'S ONLY
A GAME

Declan Burke

Declan Burke was born in Sligo in 1969.
He works as a journalist and writer. His
debut novel, *8-Ball Boogie*, was published by
Sitric Books in 2003.

As a kid I never had any time for
Celtic Football Club. This was
despite being from Sligo, the original
home of Celtic's founder, Brother
Walfrid. Mainly, I couldn't be doing
with all the sectarian nonsense. I loved
football, was interested in politics and
was fascinated by religion. But the
collision of all three poisoned any
possibility of reasonable discourse.

I went to London in the late
eighties, as so many others did, to
work on the building sites. Coming
from Sligo, London was something of
a culture shock. The frantic pace of

life, the multi-cultural interaction, the absence of anything approaching sentiment – all these I could handle. What was tough was the anonymity.

So, in London, I sold out. Bought a replica Celtic shirt as a response to the anonymity. The irony of wearing the colours of a Scottish football team to identify myself as Irish only occurred in hindsight. And it didn't work. I came home, worn out by indifference.

The following year I went abroad for the first time, flying into Turkey. The Celtic shirt came along with me. Say what you will about the sectarianism, Celtic's green-and-white hoops come second only to Brazil's canary yellow as a recognisable icon to anyone in the world who knows anything about football.

In Bodrum, a small fishing port on the southwest coast of Turkey, we ran into a group of football fans, all wearing their colours. There was a Bournemouth supporter, a Wolves fan and one wretched individual who'd grown up in Peterborough. There was also a Rangers fan, wearing the royal blue.

His friends wanted a photograph, Celtic and Rangers together. I had no problem with that. And perhaps that's where his animosity sprang from. He knew I didn't take the colours seriously. The shirt was only a cipher to me, devoid of any real meaning.

Anyway, the flash on the camera failed. We joked about how no camera could handle Celtic and Rangers together. He shook my hand leaving, but he didn't meet my eye.

The following year I went to Coleraine, to spend three years there in university. The Celtic shirt came with me, even though – or perhaps because – Coleraine is a Protestant town. I played football for the Saturday team; on my debut, a centre-half who looked a lot like a small island kicked me in the lower back and said, 'That'll do *you*, ya Fenian bastard.'

That did me just fine. I kept on playing football but developed a northern accent for the various shouts and calls required. I didn't take the abuse personally; by then I no longer considered myself Catholic, Fenian or Taig. The insults meant nothing to me.

I met a girl. She played trumpet in a marching band. One night she said, 'If my father knew I was talking to you, he'd break my knees.' She had nice knees, so we went our separate ways.

The political is always personal. I think of the Sikh who sweated beneath his snow-white turban on a Covent Garden building site; the Rangers fan in his blue on the south-west coast of Turkey; the girl playing trumpet in her Orange band.

I think of how maybe my generation of southern Irish have had it too easy. Playing fast and loose with symbols and ciphers, badges and logos, flirting with the legacy of green-and-white hooped hopes. How for us, all too often, it's only a game.

OCCASIONS
OF FAITH

Anthony Glavin

Anthony Glavin, born in Boston, is a
short-story writer, novelist, editor and
freelance journalist. His fiction titles
include *One for Sorrow, Nighthawk Alley* and
The Draughtsman and the Unicorn.

They tell a story in Glencolmcille
of an old man who, when asked
what was the first thing he
remembered, replied: 'The sound of
the dog barking at the mid-wife as she
made her way back down the lane.'
That's the kind of Donegal yarn at
which many of us would chuckle,
whereas an anthropologist might jot it
down in a notebook. Or so those like
myself, who harbour an occasional bias
against the social sciences, might like
to believe! 'I never knew an anthropologist to refuse a free meal,' a friend

of mine once observed, and it would probably come as no surprise to him either that even the mother of all anthropologists, Margaret Mead, has had her own research lately called into question.

I've had to change my tune, however, ever since coming across what I believe is a brilliant anthropological study of rural Ireland. A study, in fact, of that same corner of southwestern Donegal where I once lived and about which I've written myself. The book in question is called *Occasions of Faith*, a wide-ranging anthropological look at Irish Catholicism, written by an Irish-speaking American Jew named Larry Taylor, who chairs the anthropology department at the National University of Maynooth. Before coming to Co. Kildare, however, Taylor lived for a number of years in the tiny Gaeltacht fishing village of Teelin, doing the field work for his study of the forces that have shaped Catholicism in southwest Donegal.

I got to know Larry Taylor in the late 1980s, a friendship marked in part by our mutual interest in the stories of Donegal. My ear was cocked for the seeds of fiction, however, whilst Larry's was attuned to intimations of anthropology. Or so it seemed at the time, though having since read his *Occasions of Faith*, I'm not so sure. For there seems to me an artistry beyond the social sciences in his exploration of local pilgrimages or *turas*, holy wells and holy rocks – what Taylor calls the 'sacred geography' of Catholicism as practised in rural Ireland. What's more, his study of the religious imagination and its interplay with language and landscape is likely to interest anyone – Catholic, Methodist or Muslim – who's ever experienced the strange power of rural Ireland and the stories attached to every rock and cranny.

The point I'm trying to make is that 'occasions of faith' are not textbook stuff for Taylor, nor necessarily, for that matter, for any of us. Take for example the story of a friend I know who visited Glencolmcille last October with his two young daughters. Having hiked up Glen Head, they descended via the holy well attributed to St Colmcille, marked by an enormous cairn. A collapsed Catholic who often ponders what alternative spiritual framework he might offer his children, my friend was somewhat taken aback when his ten-year-old daughter enquired might they say a prayer? For an older neighbour badly injured by an auto. After praying silently, they each took a sip from the well, then made their way back down the headland and eventually back to Dublin, where their neighbour would, in time, make a recovery bordering on the miraculous. Upon hearing his tale of the holy well, I told my friend to track down *Occasions of Faith*. Written by an anthropologist no less.

TRAVELLING
LIGHT

Mary Morrissy

Mary Morrissy was born in Dublin in
1957. She is the author of a collection of
short stories, *A Lazy Eye*, and two novels,
Mother of Pearl and *The Pretender*. She works
as a freelance journalist and a teacher of
creative writing.

Have you ever noticed that in films
people always travel light? In
fact, they carry around empty
suitcases. Take a look next time you see
a film, particularly those old black-
and-white ones. A graven-chinned
movie idol stands on the station
platform awaiting the arrival of his
lady love. She will always be carrying
several suitcases and our hero will
inevitably heft one of them and slot it
under his arm – for God's sake – while
swinging two more airily in either
hand. No one in the movies ever
arrives with a couple of ragged plastic

bags overflowing with dirty laundry or souvenirs that could not be stuffed into the suitcase. In movie luggage, the zips always meet in the middle; the cases do not have to be straddled and sat upon to get them closed; the wheels never fall off.

I try to pack on the weight principle, bringing only what I can easily carry. Where that principle falls down is that being cursed with a most undependable pair of feet, I always have to pack an extra pair of shoes or two, to cover the inevitable blistering of toes and chafing of heels. The other offence against travelling light is books. I invariably carry two books, at least. The fear of being stranded on a long journey or in an airport lounge without a good read is too much to bear. Already the internal green digital clock that weighs in my bags has registered several kilos before I've slung in underwear or the sweater in case it gets cold, or the ubiquitous raincoat. I envy those people who don't feel the need to pack with a view to every eventuality.

I once met a man on a bus going to Dover for a channel crossing who carried a small, old-fashioned leather suitcase that sat snugly in his lap. 'If it doesn't fit in here,' he declared stoutly tapping the age-smoothened lid of the case, 'it doesn't come with me.' I looked down at my bulging rucksack, standing in the aisle of the bus because it was too fat to go in the overhead rack, and blushed to think of all the unnecessary precautionary items packed inside.

Travel, they say, broadens the horizons. But what attracts me about travelling is the reductions it imposes. For one, you are leaving behind most of the trappings that you consider vital to conduct your everyday life. And, after a few days living out of a suitcase, you realise how little you actually need to live. And inevitably, you discover that half the things you've assiduously packed, you never use. They're only there to make you feel secure. Uselessly secure.

I think of that man on the Dover bus often. I've never managed to reduce my luggage, even to his modest proportions. But I keep it in mind. My ultimate ambition, of course, is to achieve the total Zen of travel. Just like in the movies, I want to reach the Nirvana of travelling with an empty suitcase.

SUSPENDED
BELIEF

Martin Drury

Martin Drury is a theatre director and arts
consultant whose jobs include Education
Officer of the Arts Council; author of *The
Dublin Arts Report*; Founder-Director of The
Ark, A Cultural Centre for Children;
Associate Director of the Abbey Theatre.

One evening last year, I fulfilled a
long-held and deeply felt fantasy:
I sat in the corner (the stage manager's
or stage director's corner, that is) from
ten to eight to ten past eight and
watched a big show go up. And I mean
a 'big show'. The opening night of
Prokofiev's *Romeo and Juliet*, performed
by the Bolshoi Ballet at the Kennedy
Centre, Washington DC. Beyond the
heavy stage curtain I could make out
the hubbub of the audience and the
familiar ebb and flow of an orchestra

tuning up. Then I heard the applause build, peak and fall away as the conductor entered, bowed and then turned to the orchestra.

On my side of the curtain the call was given to dim the houselights as, out there in the cavernous gloom, the opening strains of the music began to weave their magic. While out there was order and focus and atmosphere, my side of the curtain, though highly disciplined, was full of suppressed tension. I counted more than thirty people within my immediate eye line. There were dancers waiting in the wings, some still, as if meditating, others limbering up; stage management staff alert and whispering; and a muscular stage crew poised to pull the curtain and then fly the gauze screen which presented the opening image of a piazza in early morning mist.

Music and dance may be universal languages but that has no bearing backstage and so I watched the Bolshoi staff calling the show in Russian as their American counterparts, piloting the show with their headsets and monitors, whispered, 'Standing by LX 2.2, 3 and 3.1,' and then, 'Go on 2.2, 3 and 3.1.' By this time, by means of the music out front and the flurry of activity backstage, we were airborne and the passengers who had paid top dollar for the journey were being transported to fair Verona.

I have worked in theatre on-and-off for more than twenty years (albeit in much smaller airfields than that I have just described) but I have never lost my sense of challenge and pleasure at this moment of 'take-off'. First comes the taxiing down the runway as the audience is let into the theatre. This is followed by the pre-flight routine of checks as the performers are called from their dressing rooms to stand in the wings. Then come the final crosschecks as the doors are closed and the stage director, who will pilot the show, talks to the light and sound operators in the control tower. Finally, there is the dimming of the cabin lights as the spectators face forward, handing themselves over to the cast and crew who, ever so slowly, pull the audience away from the ground and into the higher altitude of the performance.

Aviation and theatre depend, of course, upon a vast range of very different but immensely complex human attributes and technical skills. But the 300 passengers in the jet or the 300 spectators in the theatre share a common perspective and a common and crucial role: they are charged with maintaining the willing suspension of disbelief.

And ultimately it is a matter of belief, of collective faith, the power of some communal defiance of the law of gravity, the pull of reality. That's why I've always had a liking for those plays where, like the pilot coming on the intercom for a pre-flight chat, a character addresses the audience directly at the top of the show. Best of all I like those plays when, unlike the pilot, who in his best Marlboro Man voice is really aiming to reassure the passengers, the character seems at once to establish the impossibility of the voyage to be undertaken and the absolute necessity of fastening the seatbelts on our rational selves and collectively gripping the sides of our seats. As if, through some act of collective willpower, we could achieve 'lift-off'. And we do, we do!

Right at the start of Shakespeare's *Henry V*, he has the actor playing the Chorus say:

Can this cockpit hold
The vasty fields of France?

And before we have a chance to answer 'no' and 'can we get off?', he asks us to do our bit for the cause and to:

Piece out our imperfections
With your thoughts

When it comes to the battle scenes, he requests us to:

Think, when we talk of horses, that you see them.
As never before, we live in an age where Agincourt and Verona

and a thousand other places can be brought into our living-rooms, literally at the touch of a button. And yet, for all its glories, television is really only flight simulation. The real thing is to be found at our local arts airfields, big or small, where most nights at 8 p.m. some flight of fancy begins to taxi down the runway of our collective imagination.

SUBURBAN IDYLL

Leland Bardwell

Leland Bardwell grew up in Leixlip, Co. Kildare, and was educated in Dublin and as a mature student in London. *Mother to a Stranger* is the latest of five novels and she has also written plays, radio drama and published four collections of poems including *Dosteyevsky's Grave*. She now lives in Co. Sligo.

I am being ironic. The suburb in which I found myself was far from idyllic.

In 1981, I was evicted from the small house I rented in a lane behind Adelaide Road. The landlady wanted to sell the property and in no way had I the wherewithal to buy it from her.

So, there I was with three adolescent sons with nowhere to go. So, I had no choice but to throw myself under the aegis of Dublin Corporation.

Around this time what was known

as Tallaght was spreading into the foothills of the Dublin Mountains. New housing estates – Killenarden, Fettercain, Jobstown – were mushrooming out into the hinterlands and the old buildings in the city were being demolished to give way to offices. Fine old Georgian houses were being knocked down overnight.

So, every week I queued in the corporation buildings, with hundreds of others, mostly in the same boat as I was, all of whom begged not to be sent out to Tallaght or Coolock. Strong men wept and babies howled. We executed *danses macabres*, but all to no avail. I was told that when finally my furniture was out on the street, we'd be given the key to our new abode.

When the sheriff came, riding on his Honda 50, he furnished me with my eviction papers.

I do not wish to go into the inconvenience caused to my family by this move, with the secondary school the other side of Dublin, no jobs for young people if you gave that address, no public transport, no telephones. Nor do I want to go into my own feelings of disorientation. But what saddened me most was the fate of the young married women who had been uprooted from their families, their neighbours, especially their mothers. These young women, already burdened with one or two children and a husband out of work, were suddenly expected to settle in these half-built surroundings bereft of all other human contact. Even the travellers, of whom there were many all around, with their horses and jalopies, seemed happier and ironically more settled with their freedom of movement.

When the snows came that January the roofs leaked, the houses, sub-contracted by the Corpo, were unable to stand up to this type of weather and mud ran down from the hills.

With great difficulty and many weeks of queuing at head office, I managed to get an exchange back into Dublin, but most of these poor families, unable for the fight, remained.

A few years after I left, still saddened by the memory of it all, I wrote this poem for them.

Them's Your Mammy's Pills.

They'd scraped the topsoil off the gardens
And every step or two they'd hurled a concrete block
Bolsters of mud like hippos from the hills
Rolled on the planters' plantings of the riff raff of the city.

The schizophrenic planners had finished off their job
Folded their papers, put away their pens
The city clearances were well ahead.

And all day long a single child was crying
While his father shouted, 'Don't touch them,
Them's your Mammy's pills.'

I set to work with zeal to play, 'doll's house'
'Doll's life', 'doll's garden'
While my adolescent sons played music
In the living room out front
And drowned the opera of admonitions
'Don't touch them, them's your Mammy's pills.'

Fragile as needles the women wander forth
Laddered with kids, the unborn one out front
To forge the mile through mud and rut
Where mulish earth removers rest. A crazy sculpture.

They are going back to the city for the day
That is all they live for
Going back to the city for the day.

The line of shops and solitary pub
Are camouflaged like check points on the border
The supermarket stretches emptily
A circus of sausages and time

The till girl gossips in the veg department
Once in a while a woman might come in
To put another pound on
An electronic toy for Christmas.

From behind the curtains every night
The video lights are flickering butcher blue
'Don't touch them, them's your Mammy's pills.'

No one has a job in Killenarden
Nowadays they say it is a no-go area
I wonder then who goes and does not go
In the strange, forgotten world
Of video and valium.

I visited my one time neighbour
Not so long ago. She was sitting
In the hangover position
I knew she didn't want to see me
Although she'd cried when we were leaving.

I went my way
Through the quietly rusting motor cars and prams
Past the barricades of wire, the harmony of junk
The babies that I knew
Are punk size now
And soon children will have children
And new voices ring the leit motif

Don't touch them, them's your Mammy's pills.

ACKNOWLEDGEMENTS

(In order of appearance)

GRÉAGÓIR Ó DÚILL: from *Traverse* (Lapwing, 1998), translated by the author from Irish.

CATHAL Ó SEARCAIGH: extract from 'Afterlives' by Derek Mahon reprinted by kind permission of the author and The Gallery Press, Loughcrew, Oldcastle, County Meath, Ireland. 'Poem of the Forgotten', copyright 1993 by John Haines. Reprinted from *The Owl in the Mask of the Dreamer* with the permission of Graywolf Press, Saint Paul, Minnesota.

FRED JOHNSTON: 'Boat Dreaming' from *Being Anywhere: New and Selected Poems* (Lagan Press, 2001).

MÁIRIDE WOODS: 'The Weirdness of Dead Infantas', first published in *The Stinging Fly* (summer, 2002).

MARK ROPER: 'Prayer', first published in *The Stinging Fly* (summer, 2002).

PADDY BUSHE: 'Midwife', from *Digging towards the Light* (Dedalus, 1994).

MICHEAL O'SIADHAIL: extracts from 'Uncertain' and 'Both', first published in *Our Double Time* (Bloodaxe, 1998).

LELAND BARDWELL: 'Them's Your Mammy's Pills', from *Dostoevsky's Grave* (Dedalus, 1992).

INDEX OF CONTRIBUTORS

Absalom, Mike, 244
Arrigan, Mary, 26
Bardwell, Leland, 304
Bolger, Dermot, 206
Boran, Pat, 177
Bruen, Ken, 91
Burke, Declan, 292
Bushe, Paddy, 241
Byrne, Mary J., 103
Cannon, Moya, 153
Coady, Michael, 213
Coll, Mary, 168
Connolly, Kevin, 74
Corcoran, Frank, 18
Cronin, Michael, 274
Cullen, Leo, 124
Cullen, Sylvia, 222
Cunningham, Peter, 144
Deane, John F., 97
de Fréine, Celia, 129
Denniston, Edward, 77
Deppe, Theodore, 127
Drury, Martin, 300
Duignan, Kate, 65
Dwan, Berni, 106
Falvey, Pat, 21
Fitzmaurice, Gabriel, 203
Flannery, Tony, 132

Galvin, Gerry, 41
Gébler, Carlo, 116
Glavin, Anthony, 295
Granier, Mark, 289
Hand, Rowan, 216
Hardie, Kerrie, 268
Harding, Michael, 265
Higgins, Rita Ann, 114
Hopkin, Alannah, 47
Johnston, Fred, 62
Jordan, Anthony, 112
Kearney, Joe, 228
Kelly, Eamonn, 237
Kruger, Chuck, 53
Lee, Margaret, 68
Leonard, Mae, 56
Leyden, Brian, 198
Lindsay, Nicola, 141
Logue, Rose Mary, 15
Lynch, Brendan, 271
McAughtry, Sam, 119
MacConnell, Mickey, 250
MacCurtain, Marguerite, 35
McDonnell, Gerry, 231
McGovern, Iggy, 156
Marshall, Frank, 200
Mills, Geraldine, 122
Mok, Judith, 171

Morrison, Danny, 253
Morrissey, Eamon, 279
Morrissy, Mary, 298
Mulhall, Daniel, 219
Mulvihill, Mary, 234
Murtagh, Michael, 94
Ní Chonchuir, Nuala, 12
Ní Riain, Noirín, 256
Nolan, Patricia, 165
O'Callaghan, Conor, 135
Ó Catháin, Éamonn, 44
O'Donnell, Mary, 88
O'Driscoll, Ciaran, 180
Ó Dúill, Gréagóir, 6
O'Kelly, Donal, 71
Ó Riain, Seán, 147
Ó Searcaigh, Cathal, 9
O'Siadhail, Micheal, 247
O'Toole, Ellen, 195
Pakenham, Thomas, 59
Philips, Peter, 50
Quinn, John, 109
Roper, Mark, 159
Ryan, Martin, 32
Share, Bernard, 162
Somers, Dermot, 3
Swede, George, 174
Szirtes, George, 100
Thompson, Kate, 38
Tighe, Carl, 80
Treacy, Patrick, 29
Trolan, John, 225
Tullio, Paolo, 23
van de Kamp, Peter, 186

Wakeman, John, 259
Wall, William, 262
Walsh, Thomas F., 189
Warner, Dick, 284
Whelan, G.V., 210
Wilkinson, Mary P., 138
Woods, Macdara, 286
Woods, Máiride, 85
Woods, Vincent, 183
Wyley, Enda, 281